D0572009

CALGARY PUBLIC LIBRAR

JUN - - 2015

01010101010101010101010101010

geek
knits

0101010101010101010101010101010101010101010101010101010101010

01010101010101010101 010101010

geek
knits

Over 30 Projects for Fantasy Fanatics, Science Fiction Fiends, and Knitting Nerds

Joan of Dark
aka Toni Carr

Photographs by Kyle Cassidy

 St. Martin's Griffin New York

GEEK KNITS. Copyright © 2015 by Toni Carr. Photographs © 2015 by Kyle Cassidy. All rights reserved. Printed in China. For information, address St. Martin's Press, 175 Fifth Avenue, New York, N.Y. 10010.

Designed by Susan Walsh

www.stmartins.com

The Library of Congress Cataloging-in-Publication Data is available upon request.

ISBN 978-1-250-05138-7 (trade paperback)

St. Martin's Griffin books may be purchased for educational, business, or promotional use. For information on bulk purchases, please contact the Macmillan Corporate and Premium Sales Department at 1-800-221-7945, extension 5442, or write to specialmarkets@macmillan.com.

First Edition: June 2015

10 9 8 7 6 5 4 3 2 1

FOR IRENE BASEY
AND LINDA DUNN,
WHO GAVE ME ALL
THE GEEK AND ALL
THE KNITTING

CONTENTS

Introduction   ix

THE SCIENCE FICTION GEEK   1

Companion Scarf   3
Verse Sweater   7
Bad Robot Fingerless Gloves   13
Where No Dog (or Cat) Has Gone Before   17
Communicator Purse   23
Blue Box Scarf   27
Alien Pet   31
Time Traveler Socks   37
Alien Snow Beast Balaclava   43
Fezzes Are Cool   49
Bow Ties Are Cool   53

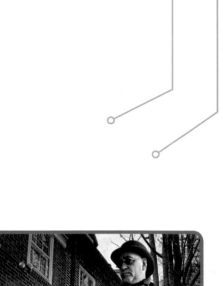

THE FANTASY GEEK   55

Helpful Worm   57
Muggle Artifact Sweater   65
Dragon   73
Intern Cowl   87
Cthulhu Fingerless Gloves   89
Poison Ivy Wrap   95
America! Sweater Dress   99

Dire Wolf   105

Dragon Rider Shrug   115

Broken Blade Hooded Sweater   119

Bunnicula   123

The Running Dead Headband and Hat   133

THE EVERYDAY GEEK   137

Baker Street Hat   139

Baker Street Scarf   143

Twenty-sided Dice Pillow   145

Eight-sided Dice Pillow   149

Six-sided Dice Pillow   151

Keep Your Pen Tie   155

Comic Book Cover   159

Chessboard Scarf   163

Acknowledgments   165

Designer Bios   167

Meet the Awesome *Geek Knits* Models!   171

Index   179

INTRODUCTION

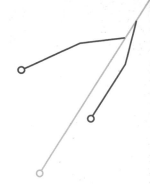

My name is Joan, and I'm a geek.

I didn't set out to be a geek. I actually spent many painful years trying to be cool, but honestly, being a geek is in my blood. I can vividly remember my mother painstakingly making the entire family matching *Star Trek: The Next Generation* uniforms (season one) to wear to a sci-fi convention. She recorded and then watched episode after episode, trying to make the uniforms perfect, right down to the invisible zipper and the piping. I was such a dork that I wasn't even aware that by all rights, as a preteen girl, I should have been mortified by this! Instead, I proudly wore it around the convention and thought it was so amazing when workers at a nearby fast food restaurant asked if we were from the TV show. I felt like the coolest kid on the planet.

When I hit my proper teenage years, I realized that my other friends hadn't had Lois McMaster Bujold and Sherlock Holmes for bedtime stories, nor did they think that weekly excursions with their dad to the comic book store was the cool thing to do. I didn't stop doing these things; I just quit telling my classmates about them. I would simply say that we took summer vacations, leaving out that they were to Worldcon in California, and hid the fact that while they were crushing on movie stars, I had the biggest crushes on Wil Wheaton and Jonathan Frakes (both with beard and without, for those wondering).

Now I've learned to publicly embrace my nerdy/dork/geeky self. I want to declare the books I read, the shows I watch, and the comics I collect in the way I dress, talk, and of course, in the way that I craft. I've learned I'm not alone in this sentiment either! I can't think of a single comic or sci-fi convention I've been to where I haven't seen at least one or two people in the audience at a panel, happily knitting away on a Who scarf or a Jayne hat.

I have been so incredibly lucky with this project. By begging friends and friends of friends or even just sending out e-mails that used the word "please" a lot, I was able to convince a lot of geek celebrities to model all the knit patterns you'll find in here. They were patient, willing, and maybe slightly bemused as they let Kyle Cassidy and me drape them in scarves, sweaters, and hats, then snap their pictures. As if they weren't all awesome enough just by being models, every celebrity in this book has picked a charity near and dear to their hearts, and we're auctioning off all the items they wore with the proceeds going to the charity of his or her choice!

This book is broken down into three sections. The Science Fiction Geek, full of patterns inspired by sci-fi; the Fantasy Geek, inspired by fantasy books, comics, and television; and finally, the Everyday Geek. These are the patterns for geeks who are geeks for chess, science, or gaming!

Speaking of gaming, the difficulty levels are inspired by gaming difficulty levels!

Easy: Patterns for the newbie! Know how to knit and purl? You can knock out these patterns!

Medium: Slightly more complex—you'll need to know how to knit, purl, increase, decrease, make basic cables, and do a little bit of color work.

Difficult: The difficult patterns mean you know everything from Easy and Medium, as well as difficult color work, such as stranded knitting, Fair Isle, and complicated cable patterns.

I hope that my fellow nerds, geeks, and dorks can find patterns in this book that will inspire them to show off their geeky selves. I've tried to include patterns from my favorite books, movies, and television shows, as well as some things that my fellow designer friends and I thought were just really cool. And by really cool, I of course, mean really geeky.

xoxx
Joan of Dark (aka Toni Carr)

THE SCIENCE FICTION GEEK

This section is inspired by the genre that believes the impossible will someday be possible! Science fiction is one of my favorite genres. It's amazing to think that these stories of space travel, aliens, or computers held in the palm of our hand could, or even already have, become true. It may not seem like science fiction and knitting go together. On one hand, we have an ages-old craft that uses simple things like wool and sticks to create clothing or toys. On the other hand, we have aliens! Space travel! Holograms! But I like to think that, much like the innovative minds that dream up our favorite science fiction stories, knitters see the realm of possibility a little broader than the average person. Knitters are dreamers and makers, and they see what many think of as hard or impossible as absolutely doable.

The patterns in this section are all inspired by this world of science fiction. There were fierce debates about some of these patterns—whether the stories they were inspired by were in fact science fiction or fantasy. What makes something science fiction? Aliens? Space travel? I was told by someone that my favorite British science fiction show is, in fact, pure fantasy, but I for one like to have that little sliver of hope that time travel and wibbly-wobbly time lines belong in the realm of science fiction possibility!

So get ready to knit your own pet alien. Dress for the cold weather as a snow beast from another planet, or simply show that you are ready to jump in a blue box and be a companion on a time-traveling adventure!

Bonnie Burton

companion scarf

By Joan of Dark

Doesn't everyone hope that someday a strange person in a blue box will show up to take them on adventures? Better make sure you're ready for him! (Honestly, it's why I run every day!) This long scarf is perfect for keeping warm, no matter what planet/dimension/continent/time you end up in. Make the matching gloves (page 4 caption) and cosplay as the eleventh Doctor's companion for a convention, a costume party, or just because!

This scarf is long, but luckily knitting it doesn't feel like you need a time machine to get to the end. It's bulky yarn on big needles, and before you know it, you'll be at the end of your scarf journey!

MATERIALS

Wool of the Andes Bulky by Knit Picks (100% Peruvian
   highland wool), 3½ ounce (100g) skeins, each
   approx. 137yd (125m)
   4 skeins in Red
Set of size 10½ (6.5mm) needles
Cable needle
Size G (4mm) crochet hook

DIFFICULTY LEVEL:
Medium

SIZES: One size

MEASUREMENTS

112" long and 7½" wide (after blocking)

GAUGE

16 stitches and 21 rows = 4"(10cm) in St st

ABBREVIATIONS

C8b: Slip 4 sts to cable needle, hold in back, knit next 4 sts, and then knit sts from cable needle.

C8f: Slip 4 sts to cable needle, hold in front, knit next 4 sts, and then knit sts from cable needle.

NOTE

With the tassels and gauge swatch, this scarf uses almost every bit of those 4 skeins. It's designed to wrap around the neck once and still hit each knee. If you're taller than 5'6"or 5'7", you might want to consider using another skein of yarn.

SCARF

Cast on 32 stitches.

Row 1: Knit across.

Row 2: K4, p to last 4 stitches, k4.

Row 3: Knit across.

Row 4: K4, p to last 4 stitches, k4.

Row 5: K4, c8f, k4, c8f, k8.

Rows 6–26: Repeat rows 2 and 3.

Row 27: Knit 8, c8b, k4, c8b, k4.

Rows 28–46: Repeat rows 2 and 3.

Repeat rows 1–46 until scarf measures 112". Bind off.

Finishing

Cut out a piece of cardboard 7 to 7½" long and wrap yarn around the cardboard about six times (or use a DVD case and wrap the yarn around the longer side). Cut across to make a bundle of yarn. Repeat to make 12 bundles total.

Starting at the corner edge of the Scarf, take the crochet hook and pull one yarn bundle through the corner, then even up the edges of the fringe and knot. Repeat evenly across, on both sides, until you have 6 tassels on each end.

Block the Scarf, and wear it on as many adventures as you can handle. And remember . . . RUN!

Love the matching gloves Bonnie is wearing? Download the pattern at www.joanofdark.com/companiongloves.

Trillian Stars

verse sweater

By Joan of Dark

Nothing in the Verse should stop you from knitting this sweater! Perfect for those moments of joyful dancing, but can also be worn when running from angry villagers. There was much debate among my friends about whether the sweater this is based on, from the all-too-quickly-canceled *Firefly,* was red or pink. So while this one is knit in pinkish tones, feel free to go for a yarn with more red tones.

If you want it really baggy, the way it was worn in the show, knit one size up. It's knit from the top down, making it easy to adjust and change the sizing as you go! This is also a great "first sweater" project, as it's supposed to look a little bit worn and crazy!

MATERIALS

Kid Seta by Plymouth Yarn (70% super kid mohair, 30% silk), 88 ounce (25g) balls, each approx. 230 yards (210m) 8 (8, 10, 10) balls in color #1011

Set of size 8 (5mm) needles

Size 8 (5mm) circular needle, 16" long

Size 8 (5mm) circular needle, 24 to 32" long

Two stitch markers

Tapestry needle

DIFFICULTY LEVEL: Medium

SIZES: Small (Medium, Large, Extra Large)

TO FIT: 32–34" (34–36, 36–38, 38–40) bust

GAUGE

17 sts and 27 rows = 4" (10cm) in St st with yarn held double

NOTE

Yarn is held double throughout.

SWEATER

Sweater Yoke

With shorter circular needle and yarn held double, cast 96 (100, 108, 116) sts. Pm and join, being careful not to twist the sts.

Rounds 1–13: Knit.

Round 14: Knit, increasing 22 (22, 24, 28) sts evenly around—118 (122, 132, 144) sts.

Rounds 15–20: Knit.

Round 21: Knit, increasing 22 (22, 24, 28) sts evenly around—140 (144, 156, 172) sts.

Rounds 22–29: Knit.

Round 30: Knit, increasing 22 (22, 22, 24) sts evenly around—162 (166, 178, 196) sts.

Rounds 31–38: Knit.

Round 39: Knit, increasing 22 (22, 22, 24) sts evenly around—184 (188, 200, 220) sts.

Rounds 40–47: Knit.

Round 48: Knit, increasing 22 (22, 22, 24) sts evenly around—206 (210, 222, 244) sts.

Rounds 49–57: Knit.

First Sleeve

With straight needles, knit 42 (44, 46, 48) sts, mark 42nd (44th, 46th, 48th) st, leave all remaining sts on circular needle.

Cast on 5 (7, 9, 9) sts, purl to end of row,

cast on 5 (7, 9, 9) sts—52 (58, 64, 66) sts.

Next Row: Knit.

Next Row: Cast on 2 (4, 4, 4) sts, purl to end of row, cast on 2 (4, 4, 4) sts—56 (66, 72, 74) sts.

Next Row: Knit.

Next Row: Purl.

Next Row: Knit.

Repeat last two rows 10 times more.

Decrease Rows

Row 1: Purl.

Row 2: K1, ssk, knit to last 3 sts, k2tog, k1—54 (64, 70, 72) sts.

Row 3: Purl.

Row 4: Knit.

Rows 5–12: Repeat rows 3 and 4.

Repeat rows 1–12 two times more—50 (60, 66, 68) sts.

Repeat rows 1–4 twice—46 (56, 62, 64) sts. Pm on last st of final row 4. Work in reverse St st (purl rows on RS, knit rows on WS) for 6" (6, 6½, 7) from this marker, ending with a knit (WS) row.

Increase Rows

Row 1: Purl.

Row 2: Knit, increasing 6 sts evenly across—52 (62, 68, 70) sts.

Row 3: Purl.

Miracle Laurie

Repeat last 4 rows twice more—64 (74, 80, 82) sts.

Continue in reverse St st until sleeve measures 13½" (14, 14½, 15) from marker.

Edge Decreases

Note: These funky decreases make the sleeve look a bit worn, as on the show. If it's not your style, simply continue in St st for 1", then bind off.

Row 1: Purl 32 (42, 48, 50), turn, leaving remaining sts on hold.

Row 2: Bind off 2 sts, knit to last 2 sts, k2tog.

Row 3: Purl.

Row 4: [K2tog] two times, knit to last 4 sts, [ssk] two times.

Row 5: [P2tog] two times, purl to last 4 sts, [ssp] two times.

Repeat rows 4 and 5 twice more.

Bind off.

Join yarn to 32 held sts.

Row 1: Purl.

Row 2: Bind off 2 sts, knit to last 2 sts, ssk.

Row 3: Purl.

Row 4: [K2tog] two times, knit to last 4 sts, [ssk] two times.

Row 5: [P2tog] two times, purl to last 4 sts, [ssp] two times.

Repeat rows 4 and 5 twice more.

Bind off.

Second Sleeve

Join yarn at marked st of First Sleeve. Knit across 61 (61, 65, 74) sts of body.

With straight needles, knit across next 42 (44, 46, 48) sts, marking the 42nd (44th, 46th, 48th) st.

Leave all remaining sts on circ needle.

Work Second Sleeve same as first.

Body

Join at marked st of Second Sleeve.

With longer circ needle, knit across remaining 61 (61, 65, 74) sts of body, cast on 14 (16, 16, 20) sts at underarm, knit across next 61 (61, 65, 74) sts, cast on 14 (16, 16, 20) sts for other underarm, knit to end, pm for beg of round—150 (154, 162, 188) sts.

Next Round: Knit, increasing 20 (22, 22, 24) sts evenly around—170 (176, 184, 212) sts.

Knit 2 rounds.

Next Round: Knit, increasing 20 (22, 22, 24) sts evenly around—190 (198, 206, 236) sts.

Knit around until piece measures 21" (24, 26, 26) from underarm cast-on (or desired length).

Bind off.

Verse Sweater Pattern

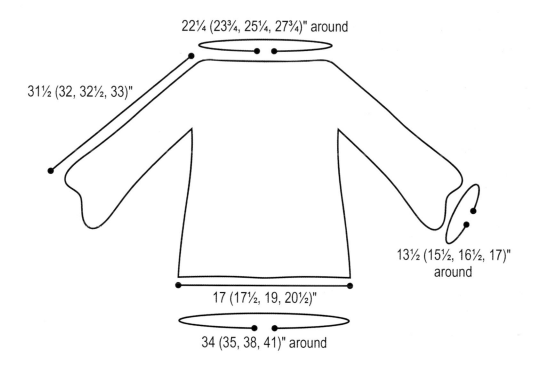

22¼ (23¾, 25¼, 27¾)" around

31½ (32, 32½, 33)"

13½ (15½, 16½, 17)" around

17 (17½, 19, 20½)"

34 (35, 38, 41)" around

Finishing

Sew sleeve seams and underarm gaps. Let the visible edging show on the Stockinette side of the work, then turn inside out so the purl side shows when worn. Weave in ends.

Donna Lynch

BAD ROBOT FINGERLESS GLOVES

By Laura Hohman

There are all sorts of bad robots in science fiction and fantasy. These gloves, however, are inspired by some British robots that have terrified children since they first appeared on television in the early 1960s! Knit in the round with some color work and bobbles, these are a great project for a knitter with a little bit of experience.

MATERIALS

Stroll Glimmer by Knit Picks
   (70% fine superwash merino wool, 24% nylon,
   5% stellina), 1¾ ounce (50g) balls, each approx.
   231 yards (211m)
   For all sizes: 1 ball in Chrome (A)
   For all sizes: 1 ball in Black (B)
Set of size 2 (2.75mm) double-pointed needles
Stitch markers
Tapestry needle

DIFFICULTY LEVEL:
Medium

SIZES: Small (Medium, Large, Extra Large)

TO FIT: 6–7" (7–8, 8–9, 9–10) hand circumference

GAUGE

32 sts = 4" (10cm) in St st

SPECIAL ABBREVIATIONS

B: Bobble: Knit in front, back, front, back, and front of same stitch—5 sts. Turn. P5, turn. K5, turn. P5, turn. K5, pull 2nd, 3rd, 4th, and 5th stitches over 1st stitch.

GLOVES

Cuff

With B, cast on 48 (54, 66, 72) sts. Divide evenly across needles and join, being careful not to twist the sts. Work in k1, p1 rib for ¾" (1, 1¼, 1½).

Body (Wrist)

p					5
p					
p					
p		B			
p					1

6   1

P = purl/stitch
B = Bobble
Blank = knit

With A, knit 5 rounds. Next round, establish chart pattern: Join B and work Chart 8 (9, 11, 12) times around. Work as a set until you have completed 4 (5, 6) repeats of the chart.

Thumb

Round 1: Using B, k 24 (27, 33, 36), pm, M1, pm, k to end of round.
Round 2: Knit.
Round 3: Using A, k to marker, sm, m1, k to next marker, m1, sm, k to end of round.
Round 4: Knit.

Note: Starting here, all stitches between markers will be knit in A.
Increase Round: Work in hand pattern to marker, sm, with A, M1, knit to second marker, M1, sm, continue in hand color pattern to end—2 sts increased.
Even Round: Work in hand pattern to marker, sm, with A, knit to second marker, sm, continue in hand color pattern to end. While continuing to work in hand color pattern, alternate increase and even rounds until there are 61 (69, 81, 89) sts. Work an increase round followed by 2 even rounds until there are 67 (75, 89, 97) sts, 19 (21, 23, 25) gusset sts between markers.
Next round: Work in pattern as set to marker, remove marker, slip gusset sts to holder, remove marker, work to end in pattern as set. 48 (54, 66, 72) sts remain for hand.

Hand Pattern

★With A, k2; with B, k1; repeat from ★ around. Repeat this round 6 (8, 10, 12) times.
Next 2 Rounds: With A, knit.
Next 3 Rounds: With B, k5 (6, 8, 9); with A, k2; with B, k10 (11, 13, 14); with A, k2; with B, k5 (6, 8, 9); on opposite side of gusset sts work with B, k5 (6, 8, 9); with A, k2; with B, k10 (11, 13, 14); with A, k2; with B, k5 (6, 8, 9).
Repeat last 5 rounds twice more.

Body (Fingers)

Continue in Hand Pattern until it is completed.

With A, knit 8 (12, 16, 20) rounds.

With B, work in k1, p1 rib for ¾" (1, 1¼, 1½).

Bind off.

Thumb

Return held gusset sts to needles. With A and starting at inside of thumb, k9 (10, 11, 12), kf&b, knit to end, pick up and knit 2 sts on inside of thumb. Distribute sts across needles and join for working in the round. 22 (24, 26, 28) sts.

Next Round: Knit.

With B, work in k1, p1 rib for ½" (½, ¾, ¾). Bind off in pattern.

Finishing

Weave in ends. Block.

Roswell

WHere NO DOG (Or caT) Has gone Before

By Elizabeth Lovick

Do you have a brave, adventurous dog? Does he search for an understanding with the squirrels and birds? Go exploring through the fence and into the neighbor's yard? Or failing all of those things, do you just want to show your love of science fiction by dressing your dog up like a character from *Star Trek*?

If you answered yes to any of these questions, then this is the dog sweater for you and your pooch! Easily adjustable to your pup's size, this will knit up just in time to transport you and your dog on a space adventure!

And yes, we know that the model is of the feline variety. There are no rules saying this sweater *has* to go on a dog. Just make sure you approach your cat very, very cautiously if you wish to dress it in a sweater!

MATERIALS

Swish DK by Knit Picks (100% superwash merino wool), 1¾ ounce (50g) balls, each approx.
123 yards (112m)
1 (1, 2, 2, 3) balls in Coal (A)
2 (3, 4, 6, 8) balls in Serrano (B)
Set of size 5 (3.75mm) needles
Set of size 6 (4mm) needles
Stitch holder or scrap yarn

DIFFICULTY LEVEL:
Medium

SIZES: Toy (Small, Medium, Large, Extra Large)

TO FIT: 18" (22, 26, 30,34) / 44cm (55, 65, 75, 85) chest

12" (16, 20, 24, 28) / 30cm (40, 50, 55, 65) back*

*NOTE: Back is very easily adjustable.

GAUGE

22 sts and 36 rows = 4" (10cm) in St st

SWEATER

With A, cast on with smaller needles 98 (118, 138, 158, 178) sts.

Row 1: K2, *p2, k2. Repeat from * to end of row.

Row 2: P2, *k2, p2. Repeat from * to end of row.

Repeat these two rows 2 (2, 5, 7, 9) times more.

Continue as follows:

Row 1: [k2, p2] 3 (4, 5, 6, 6) times, knit to last 12 (16, 20, 24, 24) sts, [p2, k2] 3 (4, 5, 6, 6) times.

Row 2: [p2, k2] 3 (4, 5, 6, 6] times, purl to last 12 (16, 20, 24, 24) sts, [k2, p2] 3 (4, 5, 6, 6) times.

Repeat these two rows once more.

Keeping the rib and St st pattern correct, add in B as follows:

Row 1: Work to last 14 (18, 22, 26, 26) sts, join B and work to end of row.

Row 2: Work 16 (20, 24, 28, 28) sts in B, join A and complete row.

Row 3: Work in A for 2 sts less than row before, join B to complete row.

Row 4: Work in A for 2 sts more than row before, join B to complete row.

Repeat rows 3 and 4 until all sts are being worked in B.

Continue in B only until the back measures 11" (14, 17, 18, 21), finishing after a RS row.

Note: You can adjust back length as necessary at this point to fit your pet.

Split for the Legs

Continue in B as follows:

Next Row (WS facing): [p2, k2] 3 (4, 5, 6, 6) times, p2. Place these sts on stitch holder or scrap yarn. Bind off 2, purl to last 16 (20, 24, 28, 28) sts. Place these stitches on stitch holder or scrap yarn. Bind off 2, [p2, k2] 3 (4, 5, 6, 6) times, p2.

Right Underbelly

Continue on these last 14 (18, 22, 26, 26) sts only.

Next Row: [K2, p2] 3 (4, 5, 6, 6) times, k2.

Next Row: [P2, k2] 3 (4, 5, 6, 6) times, p2.

Repeat these two rows until the strip measures 1" (1, 2, 3, 4), finishing after a WS row and noting the number of rows worked. Break yarn and leave sts on stitch holder or scrap yarn.

Back

Return to the center 66 (78, 90, 102, 122) sts. With RS facing, rejoin B and work the same number of rows as for right underbelly. Break yarn and leave sts on stitch holder or scrap yarn.

Left Underbelly

Return to the remaining 14 (18, 22, 26, 26) sts. Work as for Right Underbelly. Break yarn and leave sts on stitch holder or scrap yarn.

Chest

With RS facing, place all sts back on the needle. Maintaining established pattern, work across the stitches of Right Underbelly. Cast on 2 sts, work across the sts of back, cast on 2, work across the sts of Left Underbelly—98 (118, 138, 158, 178) sts. Maintaining established pattern, work a further 3 (5, 5, 7, 9) rows.

Split for the Head

Continuing in the established pattern, work 44 (53, 61, 69, 76) sts. Place these on a stitch holder or scrap yarn for the right chest. Work 10 (12, 16, 20, 26) sts and place these on a thread for the back neck. Work the remaining 44 (53, 61, 69, 76) sts.

Left Chest

On these sts only, work one row in the established pattern, then shape the neck as follows:

Row 1: With RS facing, k2tog, pattern to end of row.

Row 2: Work in established pattern.

Repeat these two rows until 39 (48, 54, 61, 67) sts remain, finishing after a RS row.

Next Row: With WS facing, bind off 14 (18, 22, 26, 26), knit to end of row.

Repeat rows 1 and 2 until 20 (23, 25, 27, 32) sts remain.

Continue straight until the work measures 2½" (3, 4, 4½, 4½) from the bind-off of the underbelly.

Bind off.

Right Chest

Return to the sts for the Right Chest. With WS facing, rejoin yarn to the neck edge and work 1 row.

Shape neck as follows:

Row 1: With RS facing, work in established pattern to last 2 sts, ssk.

Row 2: Work in established pattern.

Repeat these 2 rows until 39 (48, 54, 61, 67) sts remain, finishing after a WS row.

Next Row: With RS facing, bind off 14 (18, 22, 26, 26), knit to end of row.

Repeat rows 1 and 2 until 20 (23, 25, 27, 32) sts remain.

Continue in established pattern until the work measures 2½" (3, 4, 4½, 4½) from the bind-off the underbelly.

Bind off.

Collar

With A and RS facing, pick up and knit 22 (31, 41, 49, 52) sts from the right-side neck, knit the 10 (12, 16, 20, 26) sts from the back neck, then pick up and knit 22 (31, 41, 49, 52) sts from the left-side neck.

Row 1: P2, *k2, p2; repeat from * to end of row.

Row 2: K2, *p2, k2; repeat from * to end of row.

Repeat these two rows 2 (3, 4, 5, 5) times more.

Bind off in pattern.

Legs (make 2)

With B and larger needles, cast on 18 (26, 34, 42, 50) sts and work as follows:

Row 1: K2, *p2, k2; repeat from * to end of row.

Row 2: P2, *k2, p2; repeat from * to end of row.

Repeat these two rows for 1½" (2, 2½, 3½, 6) or to desired length.

Bind off.

Finishing

Join underbelly seam, then center chest and collar seams. Place ends of seams together and join seam across front chest. Sew leg seams. Placing the seam on the inside of each leg slit, sew the legs into the openings. Weave in all ends.

If desired, place an emblem, insignia, or badge on the shoulder.

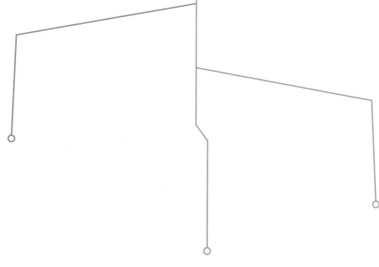

communicator purse

By Genevieve Miller

Whether you're going to a party or out to uncharted territories, this purse is a cute and functional way to carry your things. Simple on the outside, whimsical on the inside, it's lined for durability, and the strap is double-knit for strength. It's the perfect accessory for any *Trek* lover.

MATERIALS

Impeccable by Loops and Threads (100% acrylic),
4½ ounce (128g) skeins, each approx. 268 yards (245m)

    1 skein in Black (A)

    1 skein in Silver (B)

Acrylic scrap yarn in yellow, red, or blue

Set of size 8 (5mm) needles

Tapestry needle

One package black needlepoint canvas,
    containing a little less than 1 yard

About 1 yard of fabric for lining the purse

Black thread

Sewing needle

Two ¾" D-rings

One snap closure

DIFFICULTY LEVEL:
Medium

SIZES: One size

MEASUREMENTS

Approximately 6" wide by 2" deep by 8" high, excluding handle

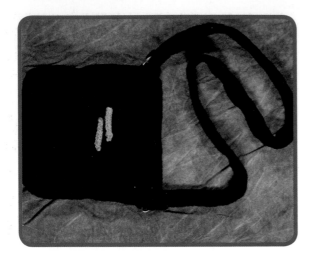

GAUGE

16 sts and 22 rows = 4" (10cm) in St st

PURSE

With A, cast on 26 stitches.

Knit in St st (K every RS row, p every WS row) for 45 rows.

Knit 46th row (WS row). (This is where the front of the Purse ends and the bottom starts. The one row of opposite stitch helps form the corner of the Purse.)

Continue knitting in St st for 12 rows.

Purl 13th row (RS row).

Starting with a WS row, continue knitting in St st for 45 rows.

Purl 46th row (RS row).

Starting with a WS row, knit St st for 12 rows.

Purl 13th row (RS row).

Starting with a WS row, knit St st for 12 rows.

Bind off all stitches.

Sides

Pick up 8 stitches along the bottom of the Purse (the 2" section between the front and the back). Knit 45 rows (or until piece measures even with the front and back pieces).

Bind off.

Repeat on the other side.

Lining

Lay the Purse upside down so the outside is facing down and the inside is facing up. Measure the front piece and cut a piece of canvas and fabric to just slightly smaller than the knit piece. Sew fabric and canvas to the back of the front piece on all four sides.

Repeat with the bottom, front, and top pieces of the bag.

Finishing

With the inside of the Purse facing out, seam the side pieces onto the main body of the purse. Carefully turn the Purse right side out.

Strap

Note: Strap is double knit for strength.
With A, cast on 8 sts.
Row 1: ★K1, bring yarn to front as if to purl, sl 1 purlwise; repeat from ★ to end.
Repeat Row 1 until Strap measures 52" or to your comfort (allow for 2" on either end to sew Strap to Purse).
Pick up 4 sts in the center of the row about 1" down from the top of each side.
Row 1: Knit.
Row 2: Purl.
Row 3: Knit.
Bind off.
Place D-ring to sit between the rows you just knit and the fabric of the Purse. Sew the bind-off row to the side of the Purse to keep the D-ring in.
Repeat on the other side.
Thread the end of the Strap under the D-ring, loop it around, and sew the end onto the Strap.
Repeat on the other side.

Silver "Handles" on Front

With B, cast on 4 stitches.
Knit an I-cord for 1½". Repeat to make a second handle.
Sew one onto the front of the bag on body and one on bottom center of flap.

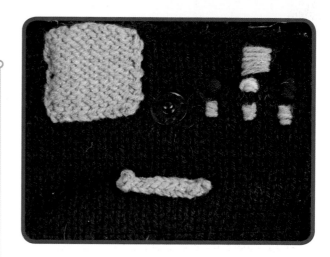

Closure

Sew a snap into the front and inside flap of the Purse, so that it will snap closed.

Embellishment

For screen
With B, cast on 12 stitches.
Knit in St st for 10 rows.
Bind off.
Sew onto front of Purse in upper left corner. (It will be covered by the flap when closed).
With B, sew on 3 "buttons" using satin stitch.
Just above, using colored scrap yarn, sew on 3 "lights" using satin stitch.
Just above, using B, sew on a small square using satin stitch.
Make sure all ends have been woven in.
Fill it with your necessities and boldly go!

René Auberjonois

BLUE BOX SCARF

By Melissa Kocias

This wibbly-wobbly scarf is just what the Doctor recommended to keep you warm and looking fashionable! It was inspired by a certain blue police callbox that can travel through time and space. Word has it that the chameleon circuit used to help it blend in with its surroundings got stuck on this particular setting, and it has retained this form ever since.

MATERIALS

Wool of the Andes by Knit Picks (100% Peruvian
   highland wool), 3½ ounce (100g) balls, each approx.
   110 yards (100m)
   3 balls in Winter Night
Set of size 9 (5.5mm) needles

DIFFICULTY LEVEL:
Easy

SIZES: One size

MEASUREMENTS

93" long and 4" wide

GAUGE

16 sts and 24 rows = 4" (10cm) in St st

SPECIAL ABBREVIATIONS

Tbl: Knit through back loop.

SCARF

Cast on 22 sts.

Row 1: Knit across.

Row 2: Purl across.

Row 3: K2, p8, k2, p8, k2.

Row 4: P2, k8, p2, k8, p2.

Row 5: K2, p2, k4 tbl 4, p2, k2, p2, k4 tbl, p2, k2.

Row 6: P2, k2, p4 tbl, k2, p2, k2, p4 tbl, k2, p2.

Row 7: K2, p2, k4 tbl, p2, k2, p2, k4 tbl, p2, k2.

Row 8: P2, k2, p4 tbl, k2, p2, k2, p4 tbl, k2, p2.

Row 9: K2, p2, k4 tbl, p2, k2, p2, k4 tbl, p2, k2.

Row 10: P2, k2, p4 tbl, k2, p2, k2, p4 tbl, k2, p2.

Row 11: K2, p8, k2, p8, k2.

Row 12: P2, k8, p2, k8, p2.

Repeat rows 1–12 41 more times. *Note:* For a longer scarf, use 4 skeins, and repeat rows 1–12 until you have reached the desired length.

Repeat rows 1 and 2.

Bind off.

Finishing

Weave in ends.

Blocking will eliminate the scalloping effect on the edges.

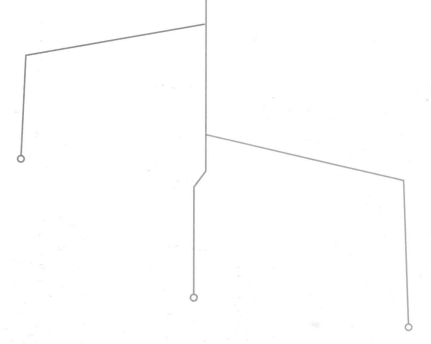

Crow T. Robot

ALIEN PET

By Mary Fitzpatrick

Who says aliens have to be gross and slimy? Make your own cute and cuddly alien that's just perfect for snuggling! Knit on large needles, then felted, this little toy is really easy to customize with different colors of yarn or googly eyes! No two aliens need look alike!

MATERIALS

Wool of the Andes by Knit Picks (100% Peruvian highland wool),
   1¾ ounce (50g) balls, each approx. 110 yards (100m)
   2 balls in Avocado
Size 13 (9mm) circular needle, 16" long
Set of size 11 (8mm) double-pointed needles
Stitch marker
Polyester fiberfill
Two ½" buttons for eyes
Tapestry needle

DIFFICULTY LEVEL:
Medium

GAUGE

10 sts and 16 rows = 4" (10cm) in St st

ALIEN

With circular needles, cast on 30 sts, pm, and join in the round. **Note:** The first row may feel a little tight.
Rounds 1–2: Knit.

Round 3: *K6, M1; repeat from *
around—35 sts.

Round 4: Knit.

Round 5: *K5, M1, repeat from * around
42 sts.

Round 6: Knit.

Round 7: *K14, M1; repeat from *
around—45 sts.

Round 8: Knit.

Round 9: *K5, M1; repeat from *
around—54 sts.

Rounds 10–11: Knit.

Round 12: K27, M1, knit to end of
round—55 sts.

Round 13: Knit.

Round 14: *K11, M1; repeat from * to end
of round—60 sts.

Rounds 15–27: Knit.

Round 28: *K8, k2tog; repeat from * to end
of round—54 sts.

Rounds 29–30: Knit.

Round 31: *K7, k2tog; repeat from * to end
of round—48 sts.

Rounds 32–33: Knit.

Round 34: *K2, k2tog; repeat from * to end
of round—36 sts.

Rounds 35–36: Knit.

Round 37: *K7, k2tog; repeat from * to end
of round—32 sts.

Rounds 38–39: Knit.

Head Fringe

Slide last 2 sts onto one size 11 dpn. Knit
2 sts from other side of size 13 needle. You
now have 4 sts on the dpn.

Work 4 sts I-cord for 10 rows.

Next Round: Knit all 4 sts as 1.

Cut yarn and pull through tail to bind off
I-cord.

Pick up 2 sts from right side of size 13
needle onto dpn. Slip needle through facing
2 sts at base of I-cord. Pick up 2 sts from
left side of size 13 needle. Join new yarn.
Knit 1 st.

Knit 2nd st and stitch from base of I-cord
together.

Knit 2nd st from base of I-cord and next st
together.

Knit last st. You now have 4 sts on the dpn.

Work 4 st I-cord for 10 rows.

Next Row: Knit through all 4 sts as 1.

Cut yarn and pull through st to bind off.

Repeat these two sections until all sts are
gone and you have 8 Head Fringes.

Arms

Smooth piece flat. Find midpoint between
top and bottom.

For left Arm, count in two rows from edge.
Starting at midpoint, pick up 6 sts vertically
with size 11 dpn. In next row toward
middle, pick up 6 sts on second needle. You

will now have 6 sts on each of two parallel needles.

Rounds 1–8: Knit.

Round 9: K1, pick up 1, k4, pick up 1, k1 on each needle—4 sts increased.

Round 10: Knit 1 row on both needles.

Round 11: K1, pick up 1, k6, pick up 1, k1. Repeat for both sides. You now have 10 sts on each needle—20 sts.

Round 12: Knit 1 row on both needles. Pick up 1 st from each needle. Knit together and bind off. Repeat across all stitches.

Repeat rounds 1–12 on the opposite side for second Arm.

Note: In this section you are knitting the two sides together to close off the end of the Arm by picking up 1 st each side to knit, then binding the st off.

Bottom

On Bottom of Alien, find center of front. Using size 11 dpns, pick up 4 sts each side of center. You now have 8 sts on your needle.

Row 1: Attach yarn and knit the 8 sts just picked up. Turn.

Row 2: Pick up next st along bottom. Purl together with 1st st. Purl across until last st. Pick up next st and purl together with last st. Turn.

Row 3: Pick up and knit next st. Knit across 10 stitches. Pick up and knit next st—12 sts. Turn.

Repeat row 2 three times, turning and knitting or purling as needed.

Next Row: Pick up next st from bottom knit together with first 2 sts. Knit to last 2 sts. Pick up next stitch from bottom. Knit together with last 2 sts.

Continue as established, knitting or purling as needed until 8 sts remain.

Next Row: Work even.

Bind off.

Feet

Find center front where front and Bottom come together. Move one stitch to right of center. Using size 11 dpn, pick up 7 sts along bottom of body. Using second needle pick up 7 parallel sts from bottom.

Attach yarn and knit 3 rows on both sides as with Arms.

Next Row: Starting on outside, k5, pick up 1, k1, pick up 1, k1. On other side, k1, pick up 1, k1, pick up 1, k5—9 sts.

Next 4 Rows: Knit.

Next Row: Starting on outside, k1, pick up 1, knit to last st, pick up 1, knit last st. Repeat on the other needle—11 sts per needle.

Knit until you have a total of 12 rows.

Bind off as with Arms.

Repeat mirrored for other Foot.

Tail

Pick up 5 sts along bottom of center back above opening. Pick up 5 sts from next row up with second needle.

Rows 1–8: Join yarn and knit on both needles as with Arms and Feet.

Row 9: K1, pick up and knit 1, k2, k2tog, turn—1st needle, 1st half of a curve row. K2tog, k2, pick up and knit 1, k1, turn—2nd needle, 2nd half of a curve row.

Rows 10–11: Knit 2 rows plain.

Repeat these 3 rows 4 times.

Next Row: Repeat Row 9.

Next Row: Knit plain.

Repeat these 2 rows 3 times.

Repeat Row 9 until tail measures 14".

Knit, reducing 1 st each needle around until 1 st remains on each needle.

Next Row: Knit last 2 sts tog, cut yarn, and pull through.

Finishing

Using tapestry needle, tuck in all ends. Felt piece. This is basically deliberately shrinking a little alien-shaped sweater. You do this by doing everything you are not supposed to do with your hair: heat, agitation, and harsh chemicals. I do this by putting the piece in a travel-size zip-closure pillow cover and then running several pieces at a time through my washer set to the smallest load size and the highest water temp. I use around 2 tablespoons of detergent. I add some mini tennis balls and cheap flip-flops to up the agitation.

This Alien was agitated for 20 minutes. When felting is finished, pull the piece into shape and let dry.

When dry, stuff to desired firmness. Sew shut with yarn and tapestry needle or with matching thread. Attach the button eyes. Using same, or contrasting, color yarn, sew in fingers and toes. I do 4 fingers and 5 toes. You can do as many as you want.

Now your Alien is ready to be loved.

The great thing about this pattern is that once you conquer it, you can change it as you like, making bigger, taller, fatter, shorter aliens as you see fit or changing color to make your Alien striped or make body parts different colors. You can also change the number and length of the individual head fringes. You can give your alien two eyes or as many as you want! You can also needle felt on the eye instead of using buttons to make your Alien baby safe.

Rodney Anonymous

time traveler socks

By Laura Hohman

Ever want to show your love for your favorite British time-traveling Doctor but don't necessarily feel like spending nine months knitting an epically long scarf? These socks are the perfect answer! Knit in classic British Doctor scarf colors, these socks are a great nod to the 1970s Baker version of the Doctor!

Easy to whip up for any knitter who has sock experience, though the first-time sock knitter shouldn't hesitate to tackle this pattern!

MATERIALS

Palette by Knit Picks (100% Peruvian highland wool),
   1¾ ounce (50g) balls, each approx. 231 yards (211m)
   For all sizes: 1 ball each in Mulberry, Gosling, Clover,
   Canary, Tomato, Serpentine, and Ash
Set of size 1 (2.25mm) double-pointed needles
Set of size 2 (2.75mm) double-pointed needles
Tapestry needle

GAUGE

32 sts and 40 rows = 4" (10cm) in St st

DIFFICULTY LEVEL:
Medium

SIZES: Small
(Medium, Large)

TO FIT: Child's 10–12
(Women's, Men's)

SOCKS

Cuff

Following striping pattern, begin Sock.
Using size 1 dpns, cast on 56 (64, 72) stitches.
Join and work in k1, p1 rib for 1" (1½, 2).

Body

Continue striping pattern on Body.
Switch to size 2 dpns and knit until Sock measures 4" (6, 8).

Heel

Choose a color that is different than the current stripe, the previous stripe, or the next stripe. The entire Heel will be knit in this color.
Knit 14 (16, 18) sts and slip 14 (16, 18) sts from previous needle onto same needle. You should have 28 (32, 36) sts on this needle.
Split remaining (instep) sts onto two needles and ignore for now.
Work Heel back and forth as:
Row 1: Sl 1, p across.
Row 2: ★Sl 1 as if to purl, k1; repeat from ★ across to end of row.
Repeat Rows 1 and 2 until Heel is 2" (2½, 3) or approximately 24 (28, 32) rows.

Turn Heel

Continue to work in solid color.
Work a series of short rows from center of Heel:
Row 1: Sl 1, p14 (16, 18), p2tog, p1, turn.
Row 2: Sl 1, k5, ssk, k1, turn.
Row 3: Sl 1, p6, p2tog, p1, turn.
Row 4: Sl 1, k7, ssk, k1, turn.
Repeat (increasing number of sts purl or knit each row), until all sts have been added to row.
There should be 17 (19, 21) sts remaining.
Finish Heel on a knit row, knitting an extra row if necessary.

Instep

Start knitting again in the striping pattern, picking up where you left off when starting the Heel.
Pick up and knit 15 (17, 19) sts on side of heel flap with spare needle.
Knit 28 (32, 36) sts (held in reserve for instep) onto second needle.
Pick up and knit 14 (16, 18) sts on other side of heel flap with third needle and knit 9 (10, 11).
Slip other 8 (9, 10) heel sts onto end of first needle.
There should be a total of 74 (84, 94) sts on 3 needles at this point: Needles 1 and 3 should have 23 (26, 29) stitches. Needle 2

should have 28 (32, 36) stitches.

Work decrease round:

Needle 1: Knit to within 3 sts of end, ssk, k1.

Needle 2: Knit.

Needle 3: K1, k2tog, k rest of stitches.

Repeat one row knit and one row decrease (working sts on needle 2 in twisted rib) until 56 (64, 72) sts remain.

Needles 1 and 3 should have 14 (16, 18) sts and needle 2 should have 28 (32, 36) sts. Knit until foot measures 2" less than desired length.

Toe

Continue to work in striping pattern.

Work decrease round:

Needle 1: Knit to last three sts, k2tog, k1.

Needle 2: K1, ssk, knit to last three sts, k2tog, k1.

Needle 3: K1, ssk, knit to end.

Work even round:

Needle 1: Knit.

Needle 2: K3, knit to least three sts, k3.

Needle 3: Knit.

Alternate decrease and even rounds until 16 (20, 20) sts remain.

Knit remaining sts from needle 1 onto needle 3.

You should now have 8 (10, 10) sts on each needle.

Striping Pattern

Color	Rows
Mulberry	2
Gosling	13
Serpentine	4
Canary	3
Tomato	6
Mulberry	2
Ash	11
Clover	6
Canary	2
Gosling	8
Tomato	4
Serpentine	2
Mulberry	3
Clover	11
Canary	3
Ash	5
Tomato	3
Gosling	8
Mulberry	3
Clover	6
Ash	4
Canary	2
Tomato	5
Mulberry	2
Serpentine	10
Gosling	3
Ash	2
Tomato	11
Canary	4
Clover	6
Mulberry	2
Gosling	11
Serpentine	3
Ash	6
Tomato	2
Mulberry	4
Gosling	2
Canary	4
Clover	14

Color	Rows
Tomato	4
Ash	4
Canary	3
Serpentine	5
Mulberry	3
Gosling	3
Ash	9
Tomato	2
Canary	4
Gosling	4
Mulberry	2
Serpentine	8
Tomato	2
Mulberry	7

Pattern is worked from the top down.

Cut 12" tail of yarn and thread onto large tapestry needle.

Hold Sock with yarn at right side, tail coming from the rear needle.

Finish Toe using Kitchener stitch:

1. Bring yarn through first front st pwise, leaving st on needle.
2. Bring yarn through first back st kwise, leaving st on needle.
3. Bring yarn through first front st kwise and slip st off needle.
4. Bring yarn through next front st pwise and leave st on needle.
5. Bring yarn through first back st pwise and slip st off needle.
6. Bring yarn through next back st kwise and leave st on needle.

Repeat steps 3–6 until all sts have been worked off needles.

Use tapestry needle to pull tail through end of Sock.

Finishing

Weave in all yarn ends.

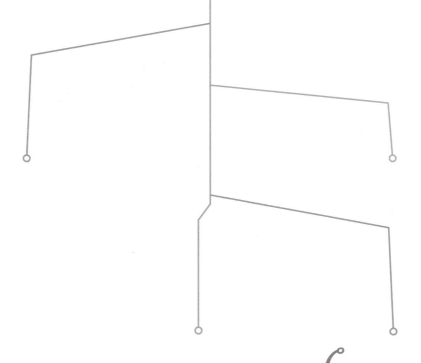

Patrick Rothfuss

ALIEN SNOW BEAST BALACLAVA

By Linda J. Dunn

When I was a kid, a certain space trilogy became my absolute favorite series and probably cemented my love of sci-fi and fantasy.

My mother created this balaclava pattern based on a snow beast on a very, very cold planet that absolutely terrified me when I was younger! You can make your own thanks to this pattern, and terrify your friends and family! (Or at the very least, keep your face warm when it's snowing and blowing outside!)

This loop stitch can be a little tricky to master, but with practice you'll find yourself whipping up these hats faster than a bounty hunter can disappear down a pit!

MATERIALS

Red Heart Supersaver (96% acrylic, 4% other fibers, 364 yards/198g)

   1 skein in White (A)

   1 skein in Mid Brown (B)

   1 skein in Coffee (C)

   1 skein in Lily Pink (D) (optional)

Size 8 (5mm) circular needle, 16" long

Set of size 8 (5mm) needles for small circumference in the round: DPNs, long circular, or 2 short circulars

Size H-8 (5mm) crochet hook

Stitch marker

Tapestry needle

DIFFICULTY LEVEL: Medium

SIZES: Teen/Adult XS (Adult Small, Adult Medium)

TO FIT: 17–19" (20–21", 22") head circumference

GAUGE

14 sts/16 rounds = 4" (10cm) in Loop st

SPECIAL ABBREVIATIONS

Pf&b (purl front and back): With yarn in front, purl without dropping st from needle, purl through the back loop, drop stitch from needle. 2 sts made from one.

LOOP STITCH

With smooth side (right side) facing, insert needle as if to knit. Place yarn over needle but instead of knitting, pull yarn down around your thumb and back over the needle. Use thumb to keep the yarn in place or switch this loop to another finger. Now knit the stitch from the needle and pull the stitch from the right needle over the knit stitch, locking the loop in place. Stop occasionally to pull the loops to ensure they are adequately tight. You can tell by looking at the reverse side of the garment if there are loose loop sts.

LOOP STITCH PATTERN

Worked in the Round:

Round 1: *Loop st, k1; repeat from * to end.
Rounds 2 and 4: Knit.
Round 3: *K1, loop st; repeat from * to end.

Worked Flat:

Row 1 (RS): *Loop st, k1; repeat from * to end.
Rows 2 and 4 (WS): Purl.
Row 3: *K1, loop st; repeat from * to end.

BALACLAVA

With circular needles and A, cast on 70 (80, 90) sts. Pm and join, being careful not to twist the sts.

Work in Loop Stitch pattern for 3½" (4, 4½), ending with an odd-numbered round.

Next Round: K 4 (3, 2), *k3tog, k 8; rep from * to end of round—58 (66, 74) sts.

Continue in pattern (starting with an odd-numbered round) until piece measures 4½" (5, 5½), ending with an odd-numbered round.

Shape Crown

Note: Change needles for working a small circumference when needed.

Next Round: Knit 4 (3, 2), *k3tog, k6; repeat from * around—46 (52, 58) sts.

Continue in pattern for another 5 rounds.

Next Round: Knit 4 (3, 2), *k3tog, k4 sts; repeat from * around—34 (38, 42) sts.

Work 5 rounds in patt.

Next Round: Knit 1 (2, 0),*k1, k2tog; repeat from * around—23 (26, 28) sts.

Next Round: Work in pattern to last 2 (0, 0)

sts, size small only end k2tog—22 (26, 28) sts.
Next Round: Knit 1 (2, 1), *k1, k2tog; repeat from * around—15 (18, 19) sts.
Next Round: Work in pattern to last 2 (0, 2) sts, k2tog 1 (0, 1) time—14 (18, 18) sts.
Next Round: K2tog around—7 (9, 9) sts.
Cut yarn, draw through remaining sts, pull tight, and secure.
You have now completed the top half of your snow beast!

Bottom Half
Back Portion
With WS facing, using circular needle and starting at start of round, pick up and purl 40 (46, 50) sts along cast-on edge, 1 stitch in every cast-on stitch. (This will take you a little more than halfway around the round.) Do not join; you will be working back and forth in rows. Pm after 20th (23rd, 25th) st.
Row (RS): Work Row 1 of Loop Stitch pattern.
Row 2 (WS): Pf&b, purl to last st, pf&b—2 sts inc.
Row 3 (RS): Work next row of Loop Stitch pattern
Repeat last 2 rows 3 (4, 4) times more, ending with a WS row—48 (56, 60) sts.

Nose Strip
Next Row (RS): Using the cable CO method, cast on 22 (24, 28) sts, work in pattern to end—70 (80, 88) sts.
Work even in pattern for 5 rows.
Next Row (RS): BO 22 (24, 28) sts, work in pattern to end—48 (56, 60) sts.

Beard Strip
Work even in pattern for 5 rows.
Next Row (RS): Using the cable CO method, cast on 22 (24, 28) sts, work in pattern to end—70 (80, 88) sts.
Work 7 rows even in pattern.
Next row, shift start of round (RS): Work in pattern to 2 sts before marker, BO 4 sts, continue in pattern as set to end of row. Do not turn, but continue working across sts in pattern to gap created by BO—66 (76, 84) sts. Start of row is now at center back.
Next Row (WS): P2tog, p to last 2 sts, p2tog—2 sts decreased.
Next Row (RS): Work Loop Stitch row as set.
Repeat above 2 rows until 30 sts remain.
Maintaining Loop Stitch, BO 2 sts at beg of each row until 2 sts remain.
Bind off.

Finishing

Sew the edges of the Nose and Beard Strips to the left side of the mask. The upper opening is for the Eyes; the lower opening is for the Mouth.

With crochet hook and color B, work 1 rnd of single crochet around lower edge.

Eyes

With crochet hook and B, starting at center bottom, work 1 rnd of single crochet around the eye opening.

At starting point, ch 7–10 sts, sl st to join to center top of eye opening.

Work around first eye opening as follows: dc around, skipping every 5th stitch; sl st to join round. Sc around again, skipping every 5th stitch. Sl st to join, fasten off.

Rejoin yarn at top of chain and work around second eye opening in the same manner.

Mouth

With crochet hook and B, starting at one corner, work 1 rnd of single crochet around the mouth opening. Sl st to join.

Next Round: Ch 3, dc around the Mouth, skipping every 5th stitch. Sl st to join. Fasten off.

Teeth

Note: Be careful to anchor into the first row of A. This is to allow the lips to hang loose in front of the Teeth for a more realistic image.

With crochet hook and A, beginning with the upper mouth and working into the first row of B, sl, ch 5, and sl st to join the round and anchor to the edge of the mouth. Single crochet into knitted row. Single crochet 3 sts to allow a gap between Teeth. Chain 6, turn and sc 6. Anchor again at end into a knitted row of the garment. Continue in above pattern, varying the length of the Teeth and the spacing as desired. Fasten off. Weave in ends.

Horns

Count 10 rows down from top of hat on side. With crochet hook and color C, anchor into 10th row and sc 20 down side of hat, then ch 10. Turn, sc 30.

Single crochet evenly across for 4 rows.

Next Row: Single crochet to last 2 sts, sc2tog. Break yarn and fasten off, leaving a 12" tail. Fold Horn in half and seam together, anchoring into side of head. Repeat to make a second Horn.

Wear when the cold gets to be too much or when you want to terrify your friends!

Drew Curtis

Fezzes are cool

By Joan of Dark

If you're the type of person to buy this book, more likely than not, you understand why fezzes are cool! Fezzes have become the latest and easiest way to cosplay. Whether at an episode viewing party or a convention, fezzes have been popping up everywhere! This pattern makes it super easy to knit your own!

This hat is done in seed stitch, starting from the bottom, then decreasing at the top, then felted. The seed stitch gives it extra thickness so that the Fez retains its shape really well.

MATERIALS

Classic Wool Roving by Patons (100% pure new wool),
   3½ ounce (100g) skeins, each approx. 120
   yards (109m)
   2 skeins in Cherry
1 skein black embroidery thread
Size 11 (8mm) circular needle, 16" long
Set of size 11 (8mm) double-pointed needles
Stitch marker
Tapestry needle

DIFFICULTY LEVEL:
Medium

SIZES: One size

MEASUREMENTS

23¼" (59cm) around after felting

GAUGE

12 sts and 20 rows = 4" (10cm) in seed st

FEZ

With circular needle and two strands held together, cast on 62 sts.

Place marker and join in the round.

Round 1: K1, p1 around.

Round 2: P1, k1 around.

Repeat these two rounds until hat measures 8" high.

Begin decrease rounds (switch to dpns when necessary):

Round 1: K2tog, p2tog, ★[k1, p1] 6 times, k2tog, p2tog; repeat from ★ to last 6 sts, [k1, p1] 4 times, k2tog, p2tog—54 sts.

Round 2: P1, k1 around.

Round 3: K2tog, p2tog, ★[k1, p1] 4 times, k2tog, p2tog; repeat from ★ to last 2 sts, k1, p1—44 sts.

Round 4: P1, k1 around.

Round 5: ★K2tog, p2tog, [k1, p1] 3 times; repeat from ★ to end of round—34 sts.

Round 5: P1, k1 around.

Round 6: ★K2tog, p2tog, [k1, p1] twice; repeat from ★ to last 2 sts, k1, p1—26sts.

Round 7: P1, k1 around.

Round 8: ★K2tog, p2tog, k1, p1; repeat from ★ to last 2 sts, k1, p1—18 sts.

Cut yarn, leaving a 12" tail.

Finishing

Thread tail through tapestry needle and pull through live stitches to close. *Note:* Don't panic if there is a tiny hole after pulling closed. It will vanish after felting.

With your tapestry needle, weave in ends very tightly so that they will not come undone during the felting process.

To felt, wash hat in hot water with soap. I usually toss my felting projects in the washing machine with an old pair of jeans to agitate and help my project felt. Check the Fez a few times toward the end of the cycle to make sure it isn't shrinking too small to fit your head!

Stuff with a towel and wrap with another towel to dry. Make sure it's shaped in the block fez shape while drying.

Take embroidery floss and cut 30 pieces to 12". Pull as many pieces as you can through eye of tapestry needle, pull through center top of hat, and loop through. Repeat until all embroidery floss is threaded through hat. Braid for 2", then knot. Trim ends until even.

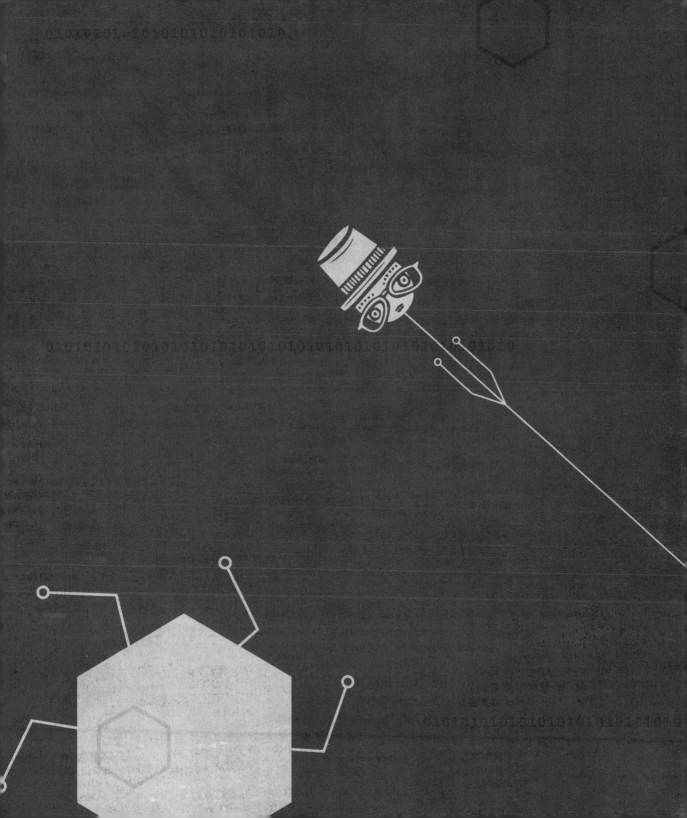

Tom Servo

BOW TIES ARE COOL

By Joan of Dark

Bow ties might be even cooler than fezzes! You certainly won't get as many strange looks when you wear them in public. They've had a pretty big comeback recently, not only from scientists on TV or British time travelers, but as part of stylish everyday office wear! (My brother has been wearing one for the past six or seven years, after an unfortunate incident with a standard necktie and a running printer.) This bow-tie pattern is also further evidence of my compulsive need to purchase sock yarn when I don't make very many pairs of socks! Also, bonus! One skein of the recommended yarn produces at least three bow ties!

Like regular neckties, I consider bow ties to be unisex. While the bow itself works for both men's and women's sizes, the actual neck section has notes on how to customize for different neck sizes.

MATERIALS

Stroll Fingering by Knit Picks (75% superwash
    merino wool, 25% nylon), 1¾ ounce (50g) balls,
    each approx. 231 yards (211m)
    1 ball in Scarlet
Set of size 2 (2.75mm) needles
Tapestry needle or small crochet hook

GAUGE

32 sts and 64 rows = 4" (10cm) in garter st

DIFFICULTY LEVEL:
Medium

SIZES: One size

SPECIAL ABBREVIATION

Kf&b: Knit front and back: Knit into the front of the next st as normal but before dropping st off, knit into the back loop of same st, then drop the st from the left needle.

BOW TIE

Cast on 26 sts.

First Bow

Rows 1–2: Knit.
Row 3: K1, ssk, k to last 3 sts, k2tog, k1—24 sts.
Repeat these three rows until 8 sts remain on your needle.
Next 2 Rows: Knit.
Next Row: K1, kf&b, k to last 2 sts, kf&b, k1—10 sts.
Repeat these three rows until 26 sts are on your needle.
Next 2 Rows: Knit.
Next Row: K1, ssk, k to last 3 sts, k2tog, k1—24 sts.
Repeat these three rows until 8 sts are on your needle.

Neck

Knit plain on 8 sts until Neck measures 16" (17, 18) or desired length. **Note:** As a girl, I made a bow tie for myself with a neck measurement of 13". That was my neck measurement plus an extra inch for tying.

Second Bow

Row 1: K1, kf&b, k to last 2 sts, kf&b, k1—10 sts.
Row 2–3: Knit.
Repeat these three rows until 26 sts are on your needle.
Next 2 Rows: Knit.
Next Row: K1, ssk, k to last 3 sts, k2tog, k1—24 sts.
Repeat these three rows until 8 sts are on your needle.
Next 2 Rows: Knit.
Next Row: K1, kf&b, k to last 2 sts, kf&b, k1—10 sts.
Repeat these three rows until 26 sts are on your needle.
Knit 2 rows.
Bind off.

Finishing

Weave in all ends with tapestry needle or crochet hook, and block.
Wear proudly, because it's just cool!

THE FANTASY GEEK

Possible? Probable? Who cares! Fantasy geeks know that they probably won't see dragons in their lifetime but still love stories about brave men and women befriending and taming them. And sure, the likelihood of a superhero fighting crime is pretty much nil, but maybe we want to dress like one anyway!

I could just be speaking for myself, but I think one of the reasons fantasy is so appealing is that it gives us that little bit of joyous escape. (Much like knitting!) Sure, I know there aren't wizards in real life. But that doesn't stop me from daydreaming that if I just take the wrong path in London, I'll end up in a certain magical alley . . .

It's a lovely bit of release from the humdrum of the everyday world. Shake off some stress and get ready for a fantastical journey with the patterns in the Fantasy section. Knit your own dragon to tame, cuddle a dire wolf, or knit the sweater that maybe, just maybe, Molly Weasley would have crafted for Arthur.

Paul and Storm

Helpful worm

By Zabet Groznaya

"Hello?" No! He said "'ello," but that was close enough. Inspired by the helpful little worm from the movie *Labyrinth,* this plush worm may not help you get to the center of Goblin City, but he will look really cute on your shelf! So kick back, make yourself a cup of tea, and knit your own plush worm toy!

MATERIALS

220 Heathers by Cascade (100% Peruvian highland wool),
   3½ ounce (100g) hanks, each approx. 220 yards (201m)
   1 hank in #9499 Beige (A)
   1 hank in #9455 Blue (B)
   1 hank in #2425 Orange (C)
Small amount black worsted weight yarn
Set of size 6 (4mm) needles
Set of size 5 (3.75mm) double-pointed needles
Polyester fiberfill
Tapestry needle
Size G (4mm) crochet hook

DIFFICULTY LEVEL:
Medium

SIZES: One size

MEASUREMENTS

11" long

GAUGE

Gauge is not essential for this project.

SPECIAL ABBREVIATIONS

Yfwd: Bring yarn forward between sts (as if to purl).

Ybk: Take yarn back between sts (as if to knit).

NOTES

The middle section and head of Mr. Worm are worked first, flat with intarsia. Be sure to always twist your yarn on the WS of the work, even if it means working some extra yfwd/ybk action between colors; it will help you to avoid an obvious seam. After seaming together his belly and noggin, you'll stuff him full of fiberfill, knit his little worm butt, and add embellishments.

WORM

Worm Belly

With A and larger needles, cast on 32 sts.

Row 1 (RS): With A, k16; with B, k16.
Row 2 (WS): With B, k16; with A, k16.
Row 3: With A, p16; with B, p16.
Row 4: With B, k16; with A, k16.
Row 5: With A, p16; with B p16.
Row 6: With B, p16; with A, p16.
Row 7: With A, p16; with B, p16.

Row 8: With B, k16; with A, k16.
Row 9: With A, p16; with B, p16.
Row 10: With B, p16; with A, p16.
Row 11: With A, p16; with B, p16.
Row 12: With B, k16; with A, k16.
Row 13: With A, k16; with B, k16.
Row 14: With B, k16; with A, k16.
Row 15: With A, p16; with B, p16.
Row 16: With B, k16; with A, k16.
Row 17: With A, p16; with B, p16.
Row 18: With B, p16; with A, p16.
Row 19: With A, p16; with B, p16.
Row 20: With B, k16; with A, k16.
Row 21: With A, p16; with B, p16.
Row 22: With B, k16; with A, k16.
Row 23: With A, k16; with B, k16.
Row 24: With B, k16; with A, k16.
Row 25: With A, p16; with B, p16.
Row 26: With B, k16; with A, k16.
Row 27: With A, k16; with B, k16.
Row 28: With B, p16; with A, p16. .
Row 29: With A, p16; with B, p16.
Row 30: With B, k16; with A, k16.
Row 31: With A, p16; with B, p16.
Row 32: With B, p16; with A, p16.
Row 33: With A, p16; with B, p16.
Row 34: With B, k16; with A, k16.
Row 35: With A, p16; with B, p16.
Row 36: With B, k16; with A, k16.
Row 37: With A, k16; with B, k16.
Row 38: With B, k16; with A, k16.

Row 39: With A, p16; with B, p16.
Row 40: With B, k16; with A, k16.
Row 41: With A, k16; with B, k16.
Row 42: With B, p16; with A, p16.

Stand Upright

To make Mr. Worm stand upright, you'll turn a short row heel over the first 16 beige (A) sts, leaving the blue (B) sts alone to deal with later.

Row 1 (RS): Wyib, slip first st. Yfwd and p14. Turn, leaving last st unknit.

Row 2 (WS): Wyif, slip first st. Ybk and k13. Turn, leaving last st unknit.

Row 3: Wyib, slip first st. Yfwd and p12. Turn, leaving last 2 sts unknit.

Row 4: Wyif, slip first st. Ybk and k11. Turn, leaving last 2 sts unknit.

Row 5: Wyib, slip first st. Yfwd and p10. Turn, leaving last 3 sts unknit.

Row 6: Wyif, slip first st. Ybk and k9. Turn, leaving last 3 sts unknit.

Row 7: Wyib, slip first st. Yfwd and p8. Turn, leaving last 4 sts unknit.

Row 8: Wyif, slip first st. Ybk and k7. Turn, leaving last 4 sts unknit.

Row 9: Wyib, slip first st. Yfwd and p5. Sl 1, pick up the horizontal bar, and place it on left needle. Move the sl st back to left needle and p2tog. Turn.

Row 10: Wyif, slip first st. Ybk and k4. Sl 1, pick up the horizontal bar, and place it on left needle. Move the sl st back to left needle and k2tog. Turn.

Row 11: Wyib, slip first st. Yfwd and p5. Sl 1, pick up the horizontal bar, and place it on left needle. Move the sl st back to left needle and p2tog. Turn.

Row 12: Wyif, slip first st. Ybk and k6. Sl 1, pick up the horizontal bar, and place it on left needle. Move the sl st back to left needle and k2tog. Turn.

Row 13: Wyib, slip first st. Yfwd and p7. Sl 1, pick up the horizontal bar, and place it on left needle. Move the sl st back to left needle and p2tog. Turn.

Row 14: Wyif slip first st. Ybk and k8. Sl 1, pick up the horizontal bar, and place it on left needle. Move the sl st back to left needle and k2tog. Turn.

Row 15: Wyib, slip first st. Yfwd and p9. Sl 1, pick up the horizontal bar, and place it on left needle. Move the sl st back to left needle and p2tog. Turn.

Row 16: Wyif, slip first st. Ybk and k10. Sl 1, pick up the horizontal bar, and place it on left needle. Move the sl st back to left needle and k2tog. Turn.

Row 17: Wyib, slip first st. Yfwd and p11. Sl 1, pick up the horizontal bar, and place it on left needle. Move the sl st back to left needle and p2tog. Turn.

Row 18: Wyif, slip first st. Ybk and k12. Sl 1, pick up the horizontal bar, and place it on left needle. Move the sl st back to left needle and k2tog. Turn.

Row 19: Wyib, slip first st. Yfwd and with A, p14. Change colors as before and with B, p16.

Worm Torso

Repeat rows 4–22 of Worm Belly. (And yes, what was RS on the Belly is now WS for the Torso, and vice versa. It'll be okay—just follow the instructions and breathe.)

Reprinted here for your convenience:

Repeat Row 4 (now WS): With B, k16; with A, k16.

Repeat Row 5 (now RS): With A, p16; with B, p16.

Repeat Row 6: With B, p16; with A, p16.

Repeat Row 7: With A, p16; with B, p16.

Repeat Row 8: With B, k16; with A, k16.

Repeat Row 9: With A, p16; with B, p16.

Repeat Row 10: With B, p16; with A, p16.

Repeat Row 11: With A, p16; with B, p16.

Repeat Row 12: With B, k16; with A, k16.

Repeat Row 13: With A, k16; with B, k16.

Repeat Row 14: With B, k16; with A, k16.

Repeat Row 15: With A, p16; with B, p16.

Repeat Row 16: With B, k16; with A, k16.

Repeat Row 17: With A, p16; with B, p16.

Repeat Row 18: With B, p16; with A, p16.

Repeat Row 19: With A, p16; with B, p16.

Repeat Row 20: With B, k16; with A, k16.

Worm Head

You'll be working in St st and making a few more short rows on the beige (A) side of the work while keeping only 16 sts on the blue (B) side and working in mostly reverse St st.

Row 1 (RS): With A, k16; with B, p16.

Row 2 (WS): With B, k16; with A, p16.

Row 3: With A, k16; with B, k16.

Row 4: With B, k16; with A, p16.

Row 5: With A, k16; with B, p16.

Row 6: With B, k16; with A, p16.

Work the next few short rows on the beige (A) sts only.

Row 7: Wyib, slip first st. K14. Turn, leaving last st unknit.

Row 8: Wyif, slip first st. P13. Turn, leaving last st unknit.

Row 9: Wyib, slip first st. K12. Turn, leaving last 2 sts unknit.

Row 10: Wyif, slip first st. P11. Turn, leaving last 2 sts unknit.

Row 11: Wyib, slip first st. K11. Sl 1, pick up the horizontal bar, and place it on left needle. Move the sl st back to left needle and k2tog. Turn.

Row 12: Wyif, slip first st. P12. Sl 1, pick up the horizontal bar, and place it on left needle. Move the sl st back to left needle and p2tog. Turn.

Row 13: Wyib, slip first st. K13. Sl 1, pick up the horizontal bar, and place it on left needle. Move the sl st back to left needle and k2tog. Turn.

Row 14: Wyif, slip first st. P14. Sl 1, pick up the horizontal bar, and place it on left needle. Move the sl st back to left needle and p2tog. Turn.

Return to working both the beige (A) and blue (B) sts and repeat rows 1–6 from this section.

Reprinted here for your convenience:

Repeat Row 1: With A, k16; with B, p16.
Repeat Row 2: With B, k16; with A, p16.
Repeat Row 3: With A, k16; with B, k16.
Repeat Row 4: With B, k16; with A, p16.
Repeat Row 5: With A, k16; with B, p16.
Repeat Row 6: With B, k16; with A, p16.

Change to smaller needles. Continue working both the beige (A) and blue (B) sts while decreasing for the crown of the Worm Head as follows:

Row 1 (RS): [With A, k2tog, k2] 4 times. [With B, p2tog, p2] 4 times—12 sts of each color rem; 24 sts total.

Rows 2 and 4 (WS): Knit all B sts, purl all A sts.

Row 3: [With A, k2tog, k1] 4 times. [With B, p2tog, p1] 4 times—8 sts of each color

rem, 16 sts total.

Row 5: [With A, k2tog] 4 times. [With B, p2tog] 4 times—4 sts of each color rem, 8 sts total.

Cut B, leaving a 6" tail. Draw through remaining sts, pull tight, and secure.

Cut A, leaving a 20" tail. With WS held together, use mattress stitch to seam Worm Body from crown to tail.

Check the ends of short rows from both the Stand Upright and Worm Head sections. Use extra A yarn to tighten up any holes before proceeding.

Worm Butt

Stuff Worm as far as you can at this point, and continue adding stuffing every few rounds. If you really want your Worm to stand up easily (rather than, say, be folded, spindled, and mutilated by a toddler), add some coins, glass pebbles, actual pebbles, or some other weight to the beige (A) side of the Worm Belly while stuffing.

Go back to cast-on edge and, with A and dpns, pick up and knit 30 sts (2 sts from the cast-on edge should have been consumed in the seaming).

Round 1: Purl.
Rounds 2, 4, and 6: Purl.
Round 3: [P2tog, p1] 10 times—20 sts.
Round 5: [P2tog] 10 times—10 sts.

Cut yarn, draw through remaining sts, pull tight, and secure, making sure piece is well stuffed.

Tiny Scarf

With C and smaller needles, cast on 4 sts and knit in garter stitch until scarf reaches a suitable length for Mr. Worm. Ours was 18" long, but if your worm size varies, you'll want to customize the length and possibly the width. Bind off. Weave in ends.

Finishing

With leftover C and black yarn scraps, embroider eyes and mouth onto Mr. Worm. You may want to employ some needle sculpture techniques to help shape his chubby cheeks. You can also use these techniques to help Mr. Worm stand a little straighter, if his posture is not to your liking. With crochet hook and using a latch-hook style approach, add 3" lengths of B yarn (folded in half) along the edges where the B on Mr. Worm's back meets the A of his belly. Don't forget to add some on his head! Comb out his "hair" so that the plys separate and fray and trim as necessary so that it stands up properly.

Hide any raw ends from knitting Mr. Worm by threading them onto a tapestry needle and pulling them into his fiberfill innards. You now have a Mr. Helpful Worm! Celebrate by coming inside to meet the missus and having a nice cup of tea.

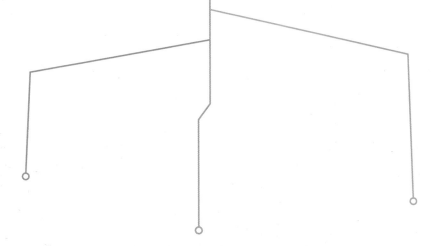

Adam Savage

Muggle Artifact Sweater

By Claire Boissevain-Crooke

"They run off eckeltricity, do they? Ah yes, I can see the plugs. I collect plugs . . . My wife thinks I'm mad, but there you are."

—Arthur Weasley, in *Harry Potter and the Goblet of Fire* by J. K. Rowling

This is a sweater I imagine Mrs. Weasley might have knit for her husband, Arthur. Even though she may not understand or approve of his fascination with Muggle Artifacts, she loves him enough to use motifs that support his enthusiasm in a special sweater for him. Artifacts become decorative elements. In this design, I included extension cords, electrical waves visible with an oscilloscope, lightbulbs, snowflakes of plugs and lightning bolts, and the technical symbol for a type of coil. This sweater does not include any automotive motifs: I am confident the flying car made Mrs. Weasley so angry she would not want to invoke its memory in this project.

This sweater is knit in the round to the armholes then worked back and forth to the shoulders. Sleeves are picked up and knit in the round from armhole to cuff. No seams! Those who prefer to steek should feel comfortable adapting the pattern to their method.

MATERIALS

Lanaloft Sport by Brown Sheep (100% wool), 1¾ ounce (50g) balls, each approx. 145 yards (132m)

5 (5, 6) balls in LL81S English Ivy (A)

1 (2, 2) ball(s) in LL01S Cottage White (B)

1 (1, 1) ball in LL78S Celery (C)

DIFFICULTY LEVEL: Hard

SIZES: Small (Medium, Large)

TO FIT: 34–36" (38–40, 42–44) chest, with approximately 3–5" ease

1 (1, 1) ball in LL585 Festival Fall (D)

1 (1, 1) ball in LL100S Wine Fire (E)

Size 3 (3.25mm) circular needle, 32" long

Size 3 (3.25mm) circular needle, 24" long

Set of size 3 (3.25mm) double-pointed needles

Size 4 (3.5mm) circular needle, 32" long

Size 4 (3.5mm) circular needle, 24" long

Size 4 (3.5mm) circular needle, 16" long

Stitch markers

Stitch holders

Tapestry needle

GAUGE

26 sts and 28 rnds = 4" (10cm) in stranded body pattern using larger needles

24 sts and 33 rnds = 4" (10cm) in sleeve pattern using larger needles

SWEATER

Body

With A and size 3 32" circular needle, cast on 256 (280, 308) sts. Pm and join, being careful not to twist the sts. Work in k2, p2 rib for 2" (2½, 2½). Change to size 4 32" needle.

Next round: Place markers for seams and patterning. Remove start of round marker; k2, pm, k62 (68, 75), pm, k1 (center front), pm, k62 (68, 75), pm for end of first half, pm, k62 (68, 75), pm, k1 (center back), pm, k62 (68, 75), pm (new start of round). 1 st rems. This will be the first st of the round. 128 (140, 154) sts each for front and back. From here, you will start the colorwork charts. Read through these instructions before you begin.

The patterning is the same on the fronts and the backs: on the lower body, work the 3 seam sts, and then the repeat across the rest of the half, taking note of which st to start the first repeat at. (Subsequent repeats will follow the chart normally; only the first repeat is changed so that the larger motifs are centered.) For the smaller pattern elements, all sizes start the repeats with stitch 4. For the larger elements, start on the stitch indicated for your size.

On the upper body, the seam sts are no longer used; simply start the repeat on the stitch indicated.

Work the charts in the following order:

Double Sine Wave: Start repeat at st 4 [17, 5].

Zigzag: Work seam element then start repeat at st 4 for all sizes.

Tesla Coil: Work seam element then start repeat at st 5 [15, 9].

Zigzag: Work seam element then start repeat at st 4 for all sizes.

Sine Wave 1: Work seam element then start repeat at st 4 for all sizes.

Zigzag: Work seam element then start repeat at st 4 for all sizes.

Plugs & Lightning: Work seam element then start repeat at st 17 [11, 4].

Zigzag: Work seam element then start repeat at st 4 for all sizes.

Sine Wave 2: Work seam element then start repeat at st 4 for all sizes.

Zigzag: Work seam element then start repeat at st 4 for all sizes.

Lightbulbs: Work seam element then start repeat at st 12 [4, 9].

Work as set until Row 7 [7, 8] of the Lightbulbs chart is complete. At this point you will divide Fronts and Back and work armhole shaping as outlined below, while continuing charts as follows:

Zigzag: Start at st 4 for all sizes.

Sine Wave 3: Start at st 4 for all sizes.

Zigzag: Start at st 4 for all sizes.

Plugs & Cords: Repeat worked on Left Front starts at st 26 (11, 17); repeat worked on Right Front starts at st 17 (19, 19).

Zigzag: Start at st 4 for all sizes.

Note: Back neck shaping for size S starts on first row of next chart.

For Size S only: Sine Wave 1: Start at stitch 4.

For Sizes M & L only: Sine Wave 4: Start at st 1 for both sizes.

Note: Back neck shaping for size M starts on Row 4 of this chart.

Note: Back neck shaping for size L starts on first row of next chart.

Zigzag: Start at st 4 for all sizes.

Row 1, RS: Bind off 6 [6, 9] sts (the 3 "seam" sts plus next 3 [3, 6] sts) at armhole edge and work in patt as set to end. Slip second half of the round to a holder for the Front. Continue only on the 128 (140, 154) sts of the Back.

Plugs & Cords

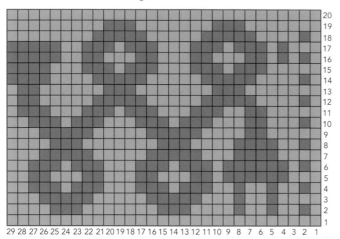

Plugs & Lightning

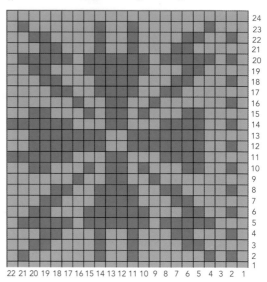

Row 2 (WS): Bind off 3 (3, 6) sts, work to end.

Bind off 2 sts at the start of the next four rows. (111 [123, 131] sts.)

Continue even until appropriate row for Back Shaping.

Next row, divide for Back neck (RS): Work 39 (42, 44) sts in patt, bind off center 33 (39, 43) sts, work to end of row. 39 (42, 44) sts each side. Working each shoulder separately, bind off 2 sts at neck edge 2 (2, 2) times, then 1 st 1 (1, 1) time. Work 3 (4, 3) rows even and place rem 34 (37, 39) shoulder sts on a holder.

Front

Return held 128 (140, 154) sts of Front to needle and rejoin yarn with RS facing. You'll pick up again on Row 8 [8, 9] of the Lightbulbs charts.

Row 1, RS: Bind off 6 [6, 9] sts (the 3 "seam" sts plus next 3 [3, 6] sts) at armhole edge and work in patt to center front marker, place this stitch on a safety pin, small holder, or length of yarn, work to end of row in pattern as set.

Row 2 (WS): Bind off 3 (3, 6) sts, work across left front sts to held center st. Join yarns and work across right front.

From here, work both sides separately.

Double Sine Wave

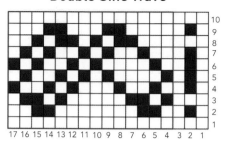

Sine Wave 1

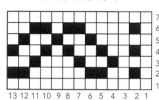

Sine Wave 2

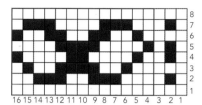

Chart Legend

- ■ Wine Fire
- ■ Ivy Green
- ■ Festive Fall
- ☐ Celery
- ■ Botanical Green
- ☐ Cottage White
- ☐ Pattern repeat

Sine Wave 3

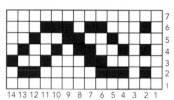

Sine Wave 4

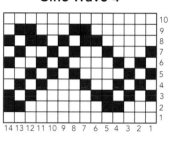

Lightbulbs

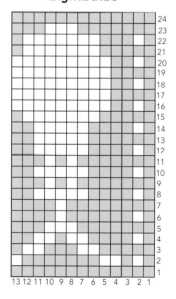

Tesla Coil

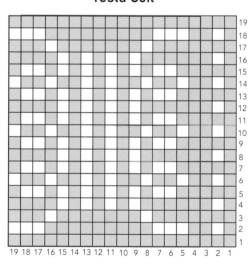

Zigzag

Bind off 2 sts at armhole edge twice, and *at the same time* decrease 1 st at neck edge every RS row 4 (10, 11) times, then every third row 17 (14, 15) times. 34 (37, 39) sts rem for each side.

Join Front to Back shoulders using 3-needle bind off.

Neckband

Weave in ends around neck edge.
With size 4 24" circular needle and A, pick up center st from holder, then 3 of every 4 sts to back of neck. Pick up 33 (39, 43) bound off st across back neck, then pick up 3 of every 4 sts to center front. Make sure that the total number of sts is divisible by 2. Pm and join. Purl 1 round.
Change to size 3 24" circular needle. Working back and forth in rows, work in k2, p2 rib for 1". Bind off. Whipstitch neckband edges to neck edge just inside purl round, left overlapping right.

Sleeves

With A and size 4 16" circular needle, pick up and knit 108 (116, 122) sts around armhole, beginning with 3 seam sts. Pm (Marker A) and join. Purl 1 round, pm at shoulder seam (Marker S) and one 3 st before Marker A (Marker B).

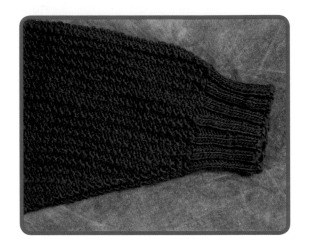

Read instructions completely before continuing.

Sleeve pattern, worked in the round
Round 1: *P1, k1; rep from * around.
Round 2: Purl.
Repeat Rounds 1 and 2 for pattern.

Sleeve pattern, worked flat
Round 1 (RS): [P1, k1] across.
Row 2 (WS): Knit.
Starting with first st of seam sts, work in sleeve pattern stitch to 6 sts past marker S, w&t.

Muggle Artifact
Sweater Schematic

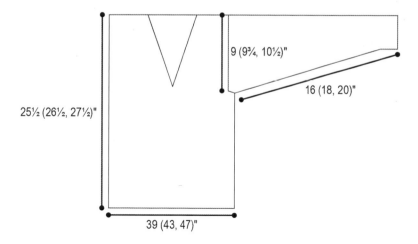

9 (9¾, 10½)"

16 (18, 20)"

25½ (26½, 27½)"

39 (43, 47)"

Work to 6 sts past Marker S, w&t. Work 6 sts past the wrapped st, knitting the st together with the wrap. Continue in this manner, working 6 sts past the previous wrapped st until there are 5 (5, 7) wraps on each side of Marker S, ending with a RS row. Continue this row to Marker A to complete sleeve cap.

Continue working in the round, in pattern stitch, for 11 (13, 17) rounds.

Decrease rounds: Slip Marker A, work 3 sts in established pattern, slip Marker B, p2tog work in established pattern to 2 st before Marker A, p2tog. Work decrease round every 5 rounds 1 (0, 4) times; every 4 rounds 19 (27, 27) times; every 3 rounds 8 (5, 0) times; and every 2 rounds 2 (0, 2) times. 48 (52, 56) sts remain.

Work even in pattern stitch as established until sleeve measures 16" (18, 20) or desired length to top of cuffs, changing to size 4 double-pointed needles when the sleeve is too small to work comfortably on a circular needle. Change to size 3 double-pointed needles. Work in k2, p2 rib for 2" (2½, 2½). Bind off loosely.

Finishing

Weave in ends. Block.
Wear with joy, celebrating the magic of electricity.

Adam Savage

Dragon

By Noel Anderson-Corwin

Ever wished you had your own dragon to raise, tame, ride into battle, or just have around to help you start a fire when camping? Well, now you can! (Okay, he won't be able to do any of those things, but he is rather cuddly!)

This dragon is simpler to knit than he appears. The slip-stitch pattern gives a scaly texture to the dragon's body and works up quickly. The body is knit from nose to tail. The horns, wings, and legs are made separately and attached to the finished body. While working the body, stuff as you knit. When knitting in the round, redistribute stitches as needed (unless otherwise specified).

Some short row shaping is used to create subtle curves; be sure to hide all wraps as you work for a smooth, clean finish.

Note: While our dragon does appear to be standing, that's just a bit of photography and placement magic. The dragon won't stand on its own.

MATERIALS

Shine Worsted by Knit Picks (60% pima cotton, 40% modal),
    1¾ ounce (50g) balls, each approx. 75 yards (68m)
    3 balls in Serrano (A)
    1 ball in Sailor (B)
    1 ball in Dandelion (C)
Set of size 3 (3.25mm) double-pointed needles
Tapestry needle
Polyester fiberfill
Two 8mm round safety eyes in blue

DIFFICULTY LEVEL:
Medium

Split stitch marker

Two red pipe cleaners (optional; not recommended if making this toy for young children)

Note: Stuff the body as you knit.

GAUGE

Gauge is not essential for this project.

SPECIAL ABBREVIATIONS

puf: With the right hand needle, pick up the float on the right side of the work and knit it together with the next stitch.

w&t: Wrap and turn.

DRAGON

Nose

With A, cast 7 sts onto one dpn.

Row 1: Purl.

Row 2: Knit.

Row 3: Purl.

Row 4: K2; work nostril [M1R, M1L, turn, p2, turn, k1, M1R, M1L, k1, turn, p4, turn, k2tog, ssk], k3; work nostril [M1R, M1L, turn, p2, turn, k1, M1R, M1L, k1, turn, p4, turn, k2tog, ssk], k2; with a second dpn, pick up 2 sts along left edge, then 2 sts along cast-on edge; with a third dpn, pick up 2 sts along cast-on edge, then 2 sts along right edge and join for working in the round—19 sts.

Body and Tail

Round 1: K1, k2tog, ssk, k1, k2tog, ssk, k9—15 sts.

Round 2: Knit.

Round 3: K1, k2tog, k1, ssk, k3, ssk, k2tog, k2—11 sts.

Rounds 4–6: Knit.

Round 7: K1, M1L, k3, M1R, k7—13 sts.

Round 8: Knit.

Round 9: K2, M1L, k3, M1R, k8—15 sts.

Rounds 10–11: Knit.

Round 12: K11, M1R, k2, M1L, k2—17 sts.

Rounds 13–15: Knit.

Round 16: K16, w&t, p6, w&t, k5, w&t, p4, w&t, k6.

Round 17: K2, M1R, k5, M1L, k5, M1L, k2, M1R, k3—21 sts.

Round 18: Knit.

Round 19: K1, yo, k2, M1R, k5, M1L, k2, yo, k11—25 sts.

Round 20: Knit.

Round 21: K3, k2tog, k5, ssk, k13.

Round 22: K2, k2tog, k5, ssk, k12.

Round 23: K21. Secure doll eyes according to manufacturer's instructions, placing the post through the eyelets created in round 19.

Round 24: K14, M1R, k4, M1L, k3—23 sts.

Round 25: Knit.

Round 26: K1, k2tog, k1, sl2tog, k1, psso, k1, ssk, k13.

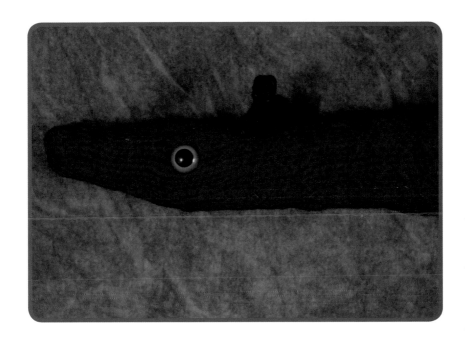

Round 27: K13, pm (this marker will now indicate the beginning of the round).
Round 28: K4, [wyif, sl 3 sts, bytb, k1] three times, k3—19 sts.
Round 29: Knit.
Round 30: K5, [puf, k3] three times, k2.
Round 31: Knit.
Round 32: K2, [wyif, sl 3 sts, bytb, k1] four times, k1.
Round 33: Knit.
Round 34: K3, [puf, k3] four times.
Round 35: Knit.
Round 36: M1L, [wyif, sl 3 sts, bytb, k1] four times, wyif, sl 3 sts, bytb, M1R—21 sts.
Round 37: Knit.

Round 38: K2, [puf, k3] four times, puf, k2.
Round 39: Knit.
Round 40: K3, [wyif, sl 3 sts, bytb, k1] four times, k2.
Round 41: Knit.
Round 42: K4, [puf, k3] four times, k1.
Round 43: Knit.
Round 44: K1, [wyif, sl 3 sts, bytb, k1] five times.
Round 45: Knit.
Round 46: K2, [puf, k3] four times, puf, k2.
Round 47: Knit.
Round 48: K3, [wyif, sl 3 sts, bytb, k1] four times, k2.
Round 49: Knit.

Round 50: K4, [puf, k3] four times, k1.

Round 51: M1L, k21, M1R.

Round 52: K2, [wyif, sl 3 sts, bytb, k1] five times, k1—23 sts.

Round 53: Knit.

Round 54: K3, [puf, k3] five times.

Round 55: Knit.

Round 56: [Wyif, sl 3 sts, bytb, k1] five times, wyif, sl 3 sts, bytb.

Round 57: Knit.

Round 58: K1, [puf, k3] five times, puf, k1.

Round 59: Knit.

Round 60: K2, [wyif, sl 3 sts, bytb, k1] five times, k1.

Round 61: Knit.

Round 62: K3, [puf, k3] five times.

Round 63: Knit.

Round 64: [Wyif, sl 3 sts, bytb, k1] five times, wyif, sl 3 sts, bytb.

Round 65: Knit.

Round 66: K1, [puf, k3] five times, puf, k1.

Round 67: K4, M1L, k5, M1R, k5, M1L, k5, M1R, k4.

Round 68: [Wyif, sl 3 sts, bytb, k1] six times, wyif, sl 3 sts, bytb—27 sts.

Round 69: Knit.

Round 70: K1, [puf, k3] six times, puf, k1.

Round 71: Knit.

Round 72: K2, [wyif, sl 3 sts, bytb, k1] six times, k1.

Round 73: Knit.

Round 74: K3, [puf, k3] six times.

Round 75: K5, M1L, k5, M1R, k7, M1L, k5, M1R, k5.

Round 76: K2, [wyif, sl 3 sts, bytb, k1] seven times, k1—31 sts.

Round 77: Knit.

Round 78: K3, [puf, k3] seven times.

Round 79: K6, M1R, k6, M1L, k7, M1R, k6, M1L, k6.

Round 80: K2, [wyif, sl 3 sts, bytb, k1] eight times, k1—35 sts.

Round 81: Knit.

Round 82: K3, [puf, k3] eight times.

Round 83: Knit.

Round 84: [Wyif, sl 3 sts, bytb, k1] eight times, wyif, sl 3 sts, bytb.

Round 85: Knit.

Round 86: K1, [puf, k3] eight times, puf, k1.

Round 87: K9, M1L, k4, M1L, k9, M1R, k4, M1R, k9.

Round 88: [Wyif, sl 3 sts, bytb, k1] nine times, wyif, sl 3 sts, bytb—39 sts.

Round 89: Knit.

Round 90: K1, [puf, k3] nine times, puf, k1.

Round 91: K10, M1L, k5, M1L, k9, M1R, k5, M1R, k10.

Round 92: [Wyif, sl 3 sts, bytb, k1] ten times, wyif, sl 3 sts, bytb—43 sts.

Round 93: Knit.

Round 94: K1, [puf, k3] ten times, puf, k1.

Round 95: K11, M1L, k5, M1L, k11, M1R,

k5, M1R, k11.

Round 96: [Wyif, sl 3 sts, bytb, k1] eleven times, wyif, sl 3 sts, bytb—47 sts.

Round 97: Knit.

Round 98: K1, [puf, k3] eleven times, puf, k1.

Round 99: K12, M1L, k5, M1L, k13, M1R, k5, M1R, k12.

Round 100: [Wyif, sl 3 sts, bytb, k1] twelve times, wyif, sl 3 sts, bytb—51 sts.

Round 101: Knit.

Round 102: K1, [puf, k3] twelve times, puf, k1.

Round 103: Knit.

Round 104: K2, [wyif, sl 3 sts, bytb, k1] twelve times, w&t, p49, w&t, k2, [puf, k3] twelve times.

Round 105: Knit.

Round 106: [Wyif, sl 3 sts, bytb, k1] twelve times, wyif, sl 3 sts, bytb.

Round 107: Knit.

Round 108: K1, [puf, k3] twelve times, puf, k1.

Round 109: Knit.

Round 110: K2, [wyif, sl 3 sts, bytb, k1] twelve times, w&t, p49, w&t, k2, [puf, k3] twelve times.

Round 111: Knit.

Round 112: Knit.

Round 113: [Wyif, sl 3 sts, bytb, k1] twelve times, wyif, sl 3 sts, bytb.

Round 114: Knit.

Round 115: K1, [puf, k3] twelve times, puf, k1.

Round 116: Knit.

Round 117: K2, [wyif, sl 3 sts, bytb, k1] twelve times, w&t, p49, w&t, k2, [puf, k3] twelve times.

Round 118: Knit.

Round 119: [Wyif, sl 3 sts, bytb, k1] twelve times, wyif, sl 3 sts, bytb.

Round 120: Knit.

Round 121: K1, [puf, k3] twelve times, puf, k1.

Round 122: Knit.

Round 123: K2, [wyif, sl 3 sts, bytb, k1] twelve times, w&t, p49, w&t, k2, [puf, k3] twelve times.

Round 124: Knit.

Round 125: [Wyif, sl 3 sts, bytb, k1] twelve times, wyif, sl 3 sts, bytb.

Round 126: Ssk, k47, k2tog.

Round 127: [Puf, k3] 12 times, puf.

Round 128: Ssk, k45, k2tog.

Round 129: [Wyif, sl 3 sts, bytb, k1] eleven times, wyif, sl 3 sts, bytb—47 sts.

Round 130: Knit.

Round 131: K1, [puf, k3] eleven times, puf, k1.

Round 132: Ssk, k43, k2tog.

Round 133: K1, [wyif, sl 3 sts, bytb, k1] eleven times.

Round 134: Ssk, k41, k2tog.

Round 135: K1, [puf, k3] ten times, puf, k1.

Round 136: Ssk, k39, k2tog.

Round 137: K1, [wyif, sl 3 sts, bytb, k1] ten times.

Round 138: Ssk, k5, k2tog, k23, ssk, k5, k2tog.

Round 139: K1, puf, k3, puf, k2, puf, [k3, puf] five times, k2, puf, k3, puf, k1—37 sts.

Round 140: Knit.

Round 141: Ssk, k3, k2tog, k2, [wyif, sl 3 sts, bytb, k1] five times, k1, ssk, k3, k2tog.

Round 142: Ssk, k29, k2tog.

Round 143: K7, [puf, k3] five times, k4.

Round 144: Sssk, k25, k3tog.

Round 145: K2, [wyif, sl 3 sts, bytb, k1] six times, k1—27 sts.

Round 146: Knit.

Round 147: K3, [puf, k3] six times.

Round 148: Knit.

Round 149: [Wyif, sl 3 sts, bytb, k1] six times, wyif, sl 3sts, bytb.

Round 150: Knit.

Round 151: K1, [puf, k3] six times, puf, k1.

Round 152: Knit.

Round 153: K2, [wyif, sl 3 sts, bytb, k1] six times, k1.

Round 154: Knit.

Round 155: K3, [puf, k3] six times.

Round 156: Knit.

Round 157: K4, [wyif, sl 3 sts, bytb, k1] five times, k3.

Round 158: Knit.

Round 159: K5, [puf, k3] five times, k2.

Round 160: Knit.

Round 161: K2, [wyif, sl 3 sts, bytb, k1] six times, k1.

Round 162: Knit.

Round 163: K3, [puf, k3] six times.

Round 164: Knit.

Round 165: K4, [wyif, sl 3 sts, bytb, k1] five times, k3.

Round 166: Knit.

Round 167: K5, [puf, k3] five times, k2.

Round 168: Knit.

Round 169: Ssk, [wyif, sl 3 sts, bytb, k1] five times, wyif, sl 3sts, bytb, k2tog—25 sts.

Round 170: Knit.

Round 171: K2, [puf, k3] five times, puf, k2.

Round 172: Knit.

Round 173: K3, [wyif, sl 3 sts, bytb, k1] five times, k2.

Round 174: Knit.

Round 175: K4, [puf, k3] five times, k1.

Round 176: Ssk, k21, k2tog—23 sts.

Round 177: K4, [wyif, sl 3 sts, bytb, k1] four times, k3.

Round 178: Knit.

Round 179: K5, [puf, k3] four times, k2.

Round 180: Knit.

Round 181: K2, [wyif, sl 3 sts, bytb, k1] five times, k1.

Round 182: Knit.

Round 183: K3, [puf, k3] five times.

Round 184: Knit.

Round 185: K4, [wyif, sl 3 sts, bytb, k1] four times, k3.

Round 186: Knit.

Round 187: K5, [puf, k3] four times, k2.

Round 188: Knit.

Round 189: K2, [wyif, sl 3 sts, bytb, k1] five times, k1.

Round 190: Knit.

Round 191: K3, [puf, k3] five times.

Round 192: Knit.

Round 193: Ssk, k2, [wyif, sl 3 sts, bytb, k1] four times, k1, k2tog—21 sts.

Round 194: Knit.

Round 195: K4, [puf, k3] four times, k1.

Round 196: Knit.

Round 197: K1, [wyif, sl 3 sts, bytb, k1] five times.

Round 198: Knit.

Round 199: K2, [puf, k3] four times, puf, k2.

Round 200: Knit.

Round 201: K3, [wyif, sl 3 sts, bytb, k1] four times, k2.

Round 202: Knit.

Round 203: K4, [puf, k3] four times, k1.

Round 204: Knit.

Round 205: K1, [wyif, sl 3 sts, bytb, k1] five times.

Round 206: Knit.

Round 207: K2, [puf, k3] four times, puf,

k2.

Round 208: Knit.

Round 209: K3, [wyif, sl 3 sts, bytb, k1] four times, k2.

Round 210: Knit.

Round 211: Ssk, k2, [puf, k3] three times, puf, k2, k2tog—19 sts.

Round 212: Knit.

Round 213: K4, [wyif, sl 3 sts, bytb, k1] three times, k3.

Round 214: Knit.

Round 215: K5, [puf, k3] three times, k2.

Round 216: Knit.

Round 217: K2, [wyif, sl 3 sts, bytb, k1] four times, k1.

Round 218: Ssk, k15, k2tog—17 sts.

Round 219: K2, [puf, k3] three times, puf, k2.

Round 220: Knit.

Round 221: K3, [wyif, sl 3 sts, bytb, k1] three times, k2.

Round 222: Knit.

Round 223: K4, [puf, k3] three times, k1.

Round 224: Knit.

Round 225: K1, [wyif, sl 3 sts, bytb, k1] four times.

Round 226: Knit.

Round 227: Ssk, [puf, k3] three times, puf, k2tog—15 sts.

Round 228: Knit.

Round 229: K2, [wyif, sl 3 sts, bytb, k1] three times, k1.

Round 230: Knit.

Round 231: K3, [puf, k3] three times.

Round 232: Knit.

Round 233: K4, [wyif, sl 3 sts, bytb, k1] twice, k3.

Round 234: Knit.

Round 235: K5, [puf, k3] twice, k2.

Round 236: Ssk, k11, k2tog—13 sts.

Round 237: K1, [wyif, sl 3 sts, bytb, k1] three times.

Round 238: Knit.

Round 239: K2, [puf, k3] twice, puf, k2.

Round 240: Knit.

Round 241: K3, [wyif, sl 3 sts, bytb, k1] twice, k2.

Round 242: Ssk, k9, k2tog—11 sts.

Round 243: K3, [puf, k3] twice.

Round 244: Knit.

Round 245: Ssk, k2, wyif, sl 3 sts, bytb, k2, k2tog—9 sts.

Round 246: Knit.

Round 247: K4, puf, k4.

Round 248: Ssk, k5, k2tog—7 sts.

Round 249: Knit.

Round 250: Ssk, k3, k2tog—5 sts.

Round 251: K5, then slip these remaining 5 sts onto one dpn. The tail tip is worked back and forth.

Tail Tip

With the Dragon's belly facing you:

Row 1: [P1, k1] twice, p1.

Row 2: Kf&b, k3, kf&b.

Row 3: [K1, p1] three times, k1.

Row 4: Kf&b, p1, k3, p1, kf&b.

Row 5: [P1, k1] four times, p1.

Row 6: Kf&b, k1, p1, k3, p1, k1, kf&b.

Row 7: [K1, p1] five times, k1.

Row 8: [K1, p1] twice, sl2tog, k1, psso, [p1, k1] twice.

Row 9: [K1, p1] twice, p1, [p1, k1] twice.

Row 10: K1, p1, k1, sl2tog, k1, psso, k1, p1, k1.

Row 11: [K1, p1] three times, k1.

Row 12: K1, p1, sl2tog, k1, psso, p1, k1.

Row 13: K1, p3, k1.

Row 14: K1, sl2tog, k1, psso, k1.

Row 15: P3.

Row 16: Sl2tog, k1, psso.

Cut yarn and pull through remaining loop to secure.

Horns

Worked as an I-cord. Make two.

Using B, cast on 3 sts, leaving a generous tail for sewing.

Rows 1–6: Knit.

Row 7: [Kf&b] three times.

Row 8: K6.

Cut yarn and pull end through remaining loops using tapestry needle.

Legs

Make four. Using B, cast on 12 sts, leaving a generous tail of at least 6" for sewing.

Round 1: Knit.

Round 2: Purl.

Rounds 3–10: Knit. Cut yarn.

Round 11: Attach A, knit.

Round 12: Kf&b, k10, kf&b.

Round 13: [P1, k1] seven times.

Round 14: [K1, p1] seven times.

Round 15: [P1, k1] seven times.

Round 16: [K1, p1] seven times.

Round 17: K2tog, [p1, k1] five times, p2tog.

Round 18: [P1, k1] six times.

Round 19: [K1, p1] six times.

Round 20: [P1, k1] six times.

Round 21: [K1, p1] six times.

Round 22: K2tog, [p1, k1] four times, p2tog.

Round 23: [P1, k1] five times.

Round 24: [K1, p1] five times.

Round 25: [P1, k1] five times.

Round 26: [K1, p1] five times.

Round 27: K2tog, [p1, k1] three times.

Round 28: [P1, k1] four times.

Round 29: [K1, p1] four times.

Round 30: [P1, k1] four times.

Round 31: [K1, p1] four times.

Round 32: K2tog, [p1, k1] twice, p2tog.

Round 33: [P1, k1] three times.

Round 34: [K1, p1] three times.

Bind off and cut yarn, leaving a 6" tail or longer.

Stuff lightly.

Claws

Make three per foot, twelve in total. Using C, cast on 3 sts and work as an I-cord.

Rounds 1–4: Knit.

Round 5: K3tog, fasten off.

Weave in ends.

Place 3 Claws, parallel to one another, in the open end of the Leg and sandwich them into place, leaving about ¼" of each claw exposed. Using the B tail, secure each claw in place while simultaneously sewing the foot closed.

Wings

Right Wing

Using A, cast on 4 sts and work as an I-cord.

Rounds 1–40: Knit.

Bind off.

If using pipe cleaners only:

For stiffer, poseable wings, fold one pipe cleaner in half. With the bent end, feed it through the I-cord starting at the bound-off side. Leave about 1" of pipe cleaner exposed and fold in the sharp ends. When attaching the wings to the body, push the pipe cleaner ends into the body, then sew. Set aside.

Using C, cast on 24 sts over one dpn.

Row 1: Purl.

Row 2: [*K1, p1* twice, k2] four times.
Row 3: [P2, *p1, k1* twice] four times.
Row 4: [*K1, p1* twice, k2] four times.
Row 5: P1, p2tog, *k1, p1* twice, p1, [*p1, k1* twice, p2] twice, [p1, k1] twice.
Row 6: [*K1, p1* twice, k2] three times, k1, p1, k3.
Row 7: P2, [k1, p1] twice, w&t, k2, p1, k2tog, k1, turn, p3, k1, w&t, k1, p1, k2, turn, p3, w&t, k2tog, k1, turn, bind off 4 sts, [*p1, k1* twice, p2] twice, [p1, k1] twice.
Row 8: [*K1, p1* twice, k2] twice, [k1, p1] twice, k1.
Row 9: P2, [k1, p1] twice, w&t, k2, [p1, k1] twice, turn, p2, k1, p1, k1, w&t, k1, p1, k1, k2tog, turn, p1, k1, p1, w&t, p1, k2tog, turn, bind off 4 sts, [p1, k1] twice, p3, k1, p1, k1.
Row 10: [K1, p1] twice, k2, [k1, p1] twice, k1.
Row 11: P2, [k1, p1] twice, w&t, k2, [p1, k1] twice, turn, p2, k1, p1, k1, w&t, k1, p1, k1, k2tog, turn, p1, k1, p1, w&t, p1, k2tog, turn, bind off 4 sts, [p1, k1] twice.
Row 12: [K1, p1] twice, k1.
Row 13: P2, k1, p1, wt, [p1, k1] twice, turn, p2, k1, wt, k1, k2tog.
Bind off, leaving a 10–12" tail.
Sew C wing flap to A I-cord. Begin by joining the two pieces at their tops (bind off tail of the wing flap to the cast-on end of the I-cord) and continue until both pieces are seamed together.

Left Wing
Using A, cast on 4 sts and work as an I-cord.
Rounds 1–40: Knit.
Bind off.
If using pipe cleaners, insert as for Right Wing.
Using C, cast on 24 sts over one dpn.
Row 1: Purl.
Row 2: [K2, *k1, p1* twice] four times.
Row 3: [*P1, k1* twice, p2] four times.
Row 4: [K2, *k1, p1* twice] four times.
Row 5: [*K1, p1* twice, p2] three times, k1, p1, k1, p2tog tbls, p1.
Row 6: K3, p1, k1, [k2, *p1, k1* twice] three times.
Row 7: [*K1, p1* twice, p2] three times, k1, p1, k1, p2.
Row 8: K1, ssk, p1, k2, w&t, p1, k1, p2tog tbls, p1, turn, k3, w&t, k1, p2, turn, bind off 4 sts, [p1, k1] twice, [k2, *p1, k1* twice] twice.
Row 9: [*K1, p1* twice, p2] twice, [k1, p1] twice, p1.
Row 10: [K1, p1] twice, k2, w&t, [p1, k1] twice, p2tog tbls, turn, k2, p1, k1, w&t, [k1, p1] twice, turn, k2, p1, w&t, p1, p2tog tbls,

turn, bind off 4 sts, [p1, k1] twice, k2, [p1, k1] twice.

Row 11: [K1, p1] twice, p2, [k1, p1] twice, p1.

Row 12: K1, [p1, k1] twice, k1, w&t, [p1, k1] twice, p2tog tbls, turn, k2, p1, k1, w&t, [k1, p1] twice, turn, k2, p1, w&t, p1, p2tog tbls, turn, bind off 4 sts, [p1, k1] twice.

Row 13: [K1, p1] twice, p1, turn, [k1, p1] twice, w&t, p1, k1, p2tog tbls.

Bind off, leaving a 10–12" tail.

Sew C wing flap to A I-cord so it mirrors the right wing.

Finishing

Attach the Horns to the top of the Dragon's head. Attach the Legs to the Dragon's belly area. Attach the Wings to the sides of the Dragon's body.

Weave in any remaining ends.

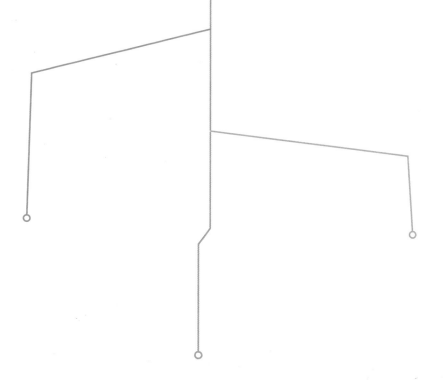

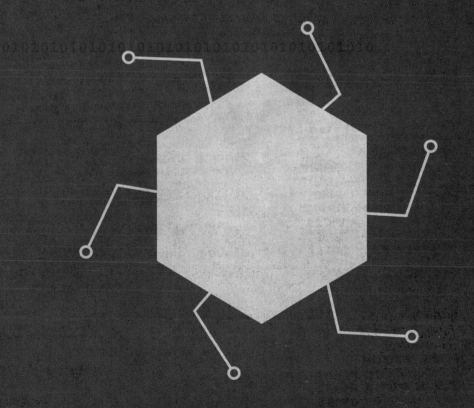

Bonnie Burton

INTERN COWL

By Joan of Dark

I adore any book, comic, cartoon, or movie having to do with superheroes. So naturally, I saw both *Thor* movies on their respective opening weekends! Being a knitter, the scarf that Darcy the intern wore in the second *Thor* movie caught my eye, and before I had even finished my popcorn, I was plotting how to make my very own!

Knit by holding two chunky weight yarns together, this scarf works up extremely quickly. Since it's an infinity scarf and loops around your neck, there are no ends to trip over when running from danger—or toward it! (Whichever way the plot takes you.)

MATERIALS

DIFFICULTY LEVEL:
Medium

SIZES: One size

Serenity Chunky Heathers by Premier Yarns
    (100% acrylic), 3½ ounce (100g) skeins, each approx.
    109 yards (100m)
    4 skeins in Smoke Heather (A)

Deborah Norville Collection Serenity Chunky by
    Premier Yarns (100% Acrylic), 3½ ounce (100g) skeins,
    each approx. 109 yards (100m)
    2 skeins in Seven Seas (B)

Set of size 19 (15mm) needles (Note: circular needles may
    be used for comfort)

Cable needle

Tapestry needle

Waste yarn for live (provisional) cast on

MEASUREMENTS

15" wide and 42" in length

GAUGE

7 sts and 11 rows = 4" (10 cm) in St st with yarn held double

NOTE

Yarn is held double throughout.

SPECIAL TECHNIQUES

Live (provisional) cast on: Tie waste yarn and working yarn together with a square knot, about 3" from end. Grasp the knot and working needle in right hand, and, similar to long-tail cast-on method, place waste yarn on index finger and working yarn around thumb on left hand.

1. Take needle behind waste yarn.
2. Move needle in front of working yarn and pick up onto needle.
3. Take needle behind waste yarn.
4. Take needle behind working yarn and pick up onto needle.

Repeat these four steps until all sts are on your needle.

COWL

With A held double and using the live cast-on method, cast on 36 sts and purl 1 row.

Row 1: *Slip 4 sts to cable needle, hold in back, k4, k4 from cable needle. Repeat three times, k4.

Row 2: Purl.

Row 3: Knit.

Row 4: Purl.

Row 5: K4, *slip 4 to cable needle, hold in front, k4, k4 from cable needle; repeat from * three times.

Row 6: Purl.

Row 7: Knit.

Row 8: Purl.

Repeat rows 1–8 three times.

Switch to B held double, work St st for 5".

With A, work St st for 6" ending with a purl row.

Switch to B, held double.

Work St st for 6" ending with a purl row.

With A:

Knit 2 rows.

Purl 1 row.

Repeat rows 1–8.

Knit 1 row.

Using tapestry needle, use Kitchener stitch to seam both sides of your scarf together. Use to keep warm in the city, which hopefully isn't being invaded by aliens or Norse gods, or involved in any sort of general mayhem.

CTHULHU FINGERLESS GLOVES

By Laura Hohman

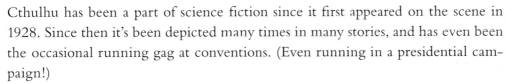

Cthulhu has been a part of science fiction since it first appeared on the scene in 1928. Since then it's been depicted many times in many stories, and has even been the occasional running gag at conventions. (Even running in a presidential campaign!)

These fingerless gloves include stranded color work and are a great way to use up sock yarn!

MATERIALS

Stroll by Knit Picks (75% superwash merino, 25% nylon), 1¾ ounce (50g) skeins, each approx. 231 yards (211m)

    1 skein in Black (A)

    1 skein in Peapod (B)

Small amount red sock yarn

Set of size 2 (2.75mm) double-pointed needles

Stitch holders

Tapestry needle

GAUGE

32 sts = 4" (10cm) in St st

DIFFICULTY LEVEL: Hard

SIZES: Medium (Large, Extra Large)

TO FIT: 7–8" (8–9, 9–10, 10–11) hand circumference

Teryl Rothery

GLOVES

Cuff

With A, cast on 54 (64, 72) sts. Divide evenly between 4 needles and join, being careful not to twist the sts. Work in k1, p1 rib for 1" (1¼, 1½).

Wrist

With A, knit 2 (8, 14) rounds.

Next Round: Join B and work Cthulhu chart across first 38 sts of round; work Star chart 2 (3, 4) times, k to end of round. Work as set until row 24 (25, 26) of Cthulhu chart is complete.

On next row, you will place markers for the thumb gusset, in the spot indicated on the chart. For size S the sts are in blue, for size M the sts are in orange, for size L the sts are in yellow. Right thumb location is marked with R, Left thumb location is marked with L.

Round 1: Work in pattern to first of two thumb stitches as marked on the chart, knit that stitch, pm, m1 with A, pm, work in pattern as set to end.

Round 2: Work even in pattern, knitting gusset sts between markers in A.

Round 3: Work in pattern to marker, sm, with A, M1, k1, M1, sm, work in pattern to end—57 (67, 75) sts.

Round 4: Work even in pattern, knitting gusset sts between markers in A.

Round 5: Work in pattern to marker, sm, with A, M1, knit to second marker, M1, sm, work in pattern to end—2 sts increased.

Round 6: Work even in pattern, knitting gusset sts between markers in A.

Repeat last two rounds until there are 67 (77, 85) sts.

Work round 5 (increase round) followed by two even rounds until there are 21 (23, 25) sts between markers, ending with an increase round. 75 (87, 97) sts total.

Next round: Work in pattern to first marker, remove marker and slip 21 (23, 25) gusset sts to scrap yarn or stitch holder; work in pattern to end of round—54 (64, 72) sts rem for hand.

Fingers

Continue in pattern until Cthulhu chart is complete, pulling tight over gussets to close gap.

With A, knit 3 (9, 15) rounds.

With A, work in k1, p1 rib for 1" (1¼, 1½). Bind off in pattern.

Star Chart

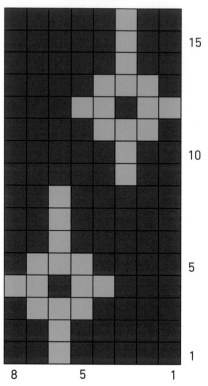

Thumb

Return held gusset sts to needles. With A and starting at inside of thumb, k10 (11, 12), kf&b, knit to end, pick up and knit 2 sts on inside of thumb—24 (26, 28) sts. Distribute sts across needles and join for working in the round.

Next Round: Knit.

With A, work in k1, p1 rib for 1" (1¼, 1½). Bind off in pattern.

Finishing

With red yarn, work duplicate stitch over eyes. Weave in ends. Block.

Cthulhu Chart

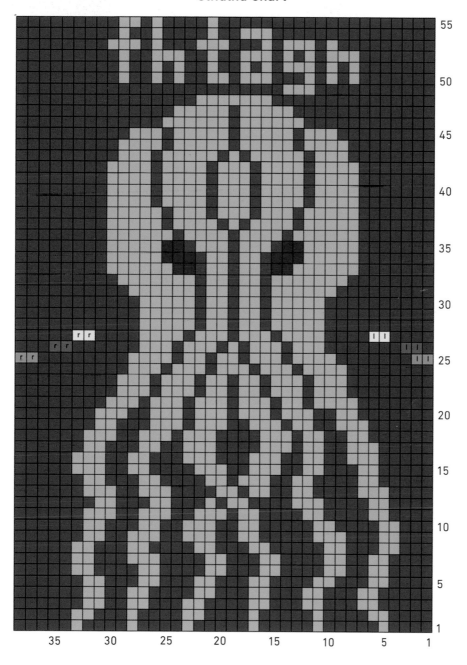

Leah Cevoli

poison ivy wrap

By Rilana Riley-Munson

This elegant lace stole is inspired by botanist Pamela Isley, the character also known as Poison Ivy. She is best known as a villain of the Batman comics and one of his more powerful foes. She was transformed into a plant-human hybrid by a science experiment gone wrong. Poison Ivy is one of the most prolific eco-terrorists. She is obsessed with plants and environmentalism. Poison Ivy uses her sex appeal, toxins from plants, and mind-controlling pheromones for her criminal activities, which are usually aimed at protecting the environment.

The deep green color and the vines and leaves in the pattern stitch make this stole a beautiful and fitting tribute to the plants that Poison Ivy loves so much.

MATERIALS

Gloss Fingering by Knit Picks (70% merino wool, 30% silk),
    1¾ ounce (50g) balls, each approx. 220 yards (201m)
    5 skeins in #24613 Jade
Set of size 7 (4.5mm) straight needles or one
    circular needle, 24" long
Eight stitch markers, two of one color to mark stitch edges,
    six of another color to mark off the pattern repeats
    (optional, but recommended)
Tapestry needle

DIFFICULTY LEVEL:
Medium

SIZES: One size

MEASUREMENTS

18" wide and 57" in length before blocking
27" wide and 80" in length after blocking

GAUGE

26 sts and 22 rows = 4" (10cm) in St st
Note: Gauge is not critical for this pattern.

PATTERN STITCHES

Seed Stitch

Row 1: *K1, p1; repeat from * to end of row.
Row 2: Purl the knit sts, knit the purl sts.
Repeat rows 1 and 2 for seed stitch pattern.

Ivy Stitch

Row 1: *K3, k2tog, k2, (yo, skp) three times, yo, k1; repeat from * to end of row.
Row 2 and all WS rows: Purl
Row 3: *K2, k2tog, k2, yo, k1, (skp, yo) three times, k1; repeat from * to end of row.
Row 5: *K1, k2tog, k2, yo, k2, (skp, yo) three times, k1; repeat from * to end of row.
Row 7: *K2tog, k2, yo, k3, (skp, yo) three times, k1; repeat from * to end of row.
Row 9: *K3, k2tog, k2, (yo, skp) three times, yo, k1; repeat from * to end of row.
Row 11: *K2, k2tog, k2, yo, k1, (skp, yo) three times, k1; repeat from * to end of row.
Row 13: *K1, k2tog, k2, yo, k2, (skp, yo) three times, k1; repeat from * to end of row.
Row 15: *K2tog, k2, yo, k3, (skp, yo) three times, k1; repeat from * to end of row.
Row 17: *(Skp, yo) three times, k1, yo, k2, skp, k3; repeat from * to end of row.
Row 19: *(Skp, yo) three times, k2, yo, k2, skp, k2; repeat from * to end of row.
Row 21: *(Skp, yo) three times, k3, yo, k2, skp, k1; repeat from * to end of row.
Row 23: *(Skp, yo) three times, k4, yo, k2, skp; repeat from * to end of row.
Row 25: *(Skp, yo) three times, k1, yo, k2, skp, k3; repeat from * to end of row.
Row 27: *(Skp, yo) three times, k2, yo, k2, skp, k2; repeat from * to end of row.
Row 29: *(Skp, yo) three times, k3, yo, k2, skp, k1; repeat from * to end of row.
Row 31: *(Skp, yo) three times, k4, yo, k2, skp; repeat from * to end of row.
Row 32: Purl.
Repeat rows 1–32 for Ivy Stitch.

WRAP

Cast on 104 stitches.
Work 4 rows in Seed Stitch.
Setup Row: Work the first 3 sts in established Seed Stitch, place edge stitch marker. Work row 1 of the Ivy Stitch pattern until 3 sts remain, place edge stitch marker. Work 3 sts in established Seed Stitch.

Next Row: Work 3 sts in Seed Stitch, slip marker, work row 2 of Ivy Stitch pattern until marker, slip marker, work 3 sts in seed stitch.

This establishes the shawl. Keep 3 sts before and after the edge markers in Seed Stitch. The Ivy Stitch pattern rows 1–32 are repeated between the markers.

Work in this fashion until the shawl measures approximately 57", ending on row 32 of Ivy Stitch pattern.

Knit 4 rows in Seed Stitch.
Bind off all sts in Seed Stitch.

Finishing

Blocking: Soak your finished shawl in lukewarm water and mild soap. Carefully squeeze out excess water and block to the measurements mentioned above.
Sew in any loose sends with a tapestry needle.

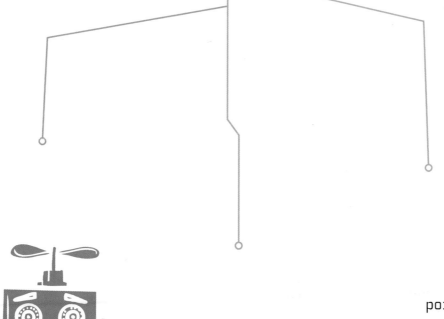

Whitney Avalon

America! Sweater Dress

By Linda J. Dunn

Who says being a hero is just for the boys? Rock this awesome patriotic sweater dress, perfect for fighting crime, going out on the town, or just hanging around the house. The cotton/linen blend yarn washes easily, so if you get it dirty kicking butt, there will be no need to panic!

This piece is started in the round, then switches to straight knitting. If you are an advanced knitter who is comfortable doing the intarsia star in the round, you can easily adjust for a more seamless knit.

Modeled by Ms. Whitney Avalon (in size medium), YouTube songstress geek whom you may have seen on *The Big Bang Theory*, in national commercials, and, well, all over the place!

MATERIALS

Cotlin by Knit Picks (70% tanguis cotton, 30% linen),
  1¾ ounce (50g) balls, each approx. 123 yards (112m)
  6 (6, 6) balls in Nightfall (A)
  3 (4, 4) balls in Moroccan Red (B)
  3 (4, 4) balls in Swan (C)
Size 6 (4mm) circular needle, 24" long
Set of size 6 (4mm) straight needles
Size 8 (5mm) circular needle, 24" long
Stitch marker
Stitch holders
Tapestry needle

DIFFICULTY LEVEL: Medium

SIZES: Small (Medium, Large)

TO FIT: 32–34" (36–38, 40–42) bust

GAUGE

24 sts and 24 rnds = 4" [10cm] in St st using smaller needles
20 sts and 24 rnds = 4" [10cm] in St st using larger needles

SWEATER DRESS

Skirt

With A and larger circular needle, cast on 200 (220, 260) sts. Pm and join, being careful not to twist the sts.

Work in k8, p2 rib until piece measures 8" (9, 10).

Begin decrease rounds:

Decrease Round 1: *Ssk, k6, p2; repeat from * around—180 (198, 234) sts.

Decrease Round 2: *K5, k2tog, p2; repeat from * around—160 (176, 208) sts.

Decrease Round 3: *K6, p2tog; repeat from * around—140 (154, 182) sts.

Decrease Round 4: *K5, p2tog; repeat from * around—120 (132, 156) sts.

Change to smaller circular needle.

Knit 2 (4, 4) rounds.

Next Round: Decrease 10 (12, 26) sts evenly around—110 (120, 130) sts.

Knit 2 rounds.

Next Round: With B, *k11 (12, 13); with C, k11 (12, 13); repeat from * around.

Begin working back and forth in rows.

Next Row (WS): Purl, keeping colors as set.
Repeat last 2 rows for 3".
Begin increase row:

Next Row (RS): With B, *k10 (11, 12), kf&b; with C, k10 (11, 12), kf&b; repeat from *—120 (130, 140) sts.

Next Row: Purl, keeping colors as set.
Work even for 2", keeping colors as set, ending with a WS row.

Next Row (RS): With B, *k11 (12, 13), kf&b; with C, k11 (12, 13), kf&b; repeat from * around—130 (140, 150) sts.

Next Row: Purl, keeping colors as set.
Work even for 1", keeping colors as set, ending with a WS row.

Next Row (RS): With A, knit, increasing 10 sts evenly across—140 (150, 160) sts.
Work 5 rows even in St st.

Next Row (RS): With A, knit, increasing 10 sts evenly across—150 (160, 170) sts.

Next Row: Purl.

Next Row (RS): K21 (24, 26), pm, k32, pm, k21 (24, 26), pm to mark end of front, k76 (80, 86) sts for back.

Work even in St st until piece measures 1½" from start of A section. Begin working chart over center 32 sts on front (between markers).

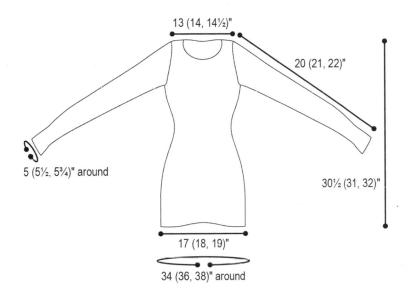

13 (14, 14½)"

20 (21, 22)"

5 (5½, 5¾)" around

30½ (31, 32)"

17 (18, 19)"

34 (36, 38)" around

Begin Star Chart

For Sizes S and L only:

Work even as set for 1", ending with a WS row.

Next row, increase (RS): K1, m1, work in pattern to 1 st before marker for back sts, m1, k to end of row. 152 (–, 172) sts; 76 (–, 86) sts each on front and back.

All sizes: Work even until piece measures 4 (4½, 4½)" from start of A section, ending with a WS row. Place 76 (80, 86) front sts on hold, continue on back sts only.

Back

Shape Armholes

Rejoin yarn at start of Front sts. Maintaining Star Chart until complete, bind off 4 sts at beg of next 2 rows—68 (72, 78) sts.

Decrease 1 st at each end of row every RS row until 60 (62, 64) sts remain. Work even until armholes measure 7½" (7¾, 8). Leave sts on hold.

Front

Note: Maintain star pattern until complete. Place held 76 (80, 86) sts on needles.

Shape Armholes

Bind off 4 sts at beg of next 2 rows—68 (72, 78) sts.

Decrease 1 st each end of row every other row until 60 (62, 64) sts remain. Work even until armholes measure 5", ending with a WS row.

Next Row (RS): K26 (27, 28), bind off 8 sts, knit to end.

Decrease 1 st at each neck edge every row until 20 (21, 22) sts remain on each side, then every other row until 15 (16, 17) sts remain on each side. Work even until piece measures same as back.

Join shoulders using 3-needle bind off, leaving center 30 sts on holder for back neck.

Neck Trim

With larger needles, pick up and knit 27 sts from left side of neck, 8 sts across front, 27 sts from right side, and 30 sts from back neck—92 sts. Pm and join.

Work in k1, p1 rib for 1". Bind off loosely in pattern.

Sleeves

With smaller straight needles and B, cast on 32 (36, 40) sts. Work in k2, p2 rib for 6", ending with a WS row.

Next Row (RS): With C, knit, increasing 6 sts evenly across—38 (42, 48) sts.

Next Row: Purl.

*Work even in St st for 1", ending with a WS row.

Next Row (RS): K1, M1, knit to last st, M1, k1—2 sts increased.

Repeat from * until there are 50 (54, 58) sts. Work even until piece measures 13". Change to A.

Repeat from * until there are 54 (58, 62) sts. Work even until piece measures 17", ending with a WS row.

Shape Cap

Bind off 4 sts at beg of next 2 rows—46 (50, 54) sts.

Decrease 1 st at each end of the next 4 rows—38 (42, 46) sts.

Decrease 1 st at each end of row every other RS row 3 (4, 5) times—32 (34, 36) sts.

Purl next row.

Bind off 2 sts at beg of next 2 (4, 6) rows.

Bind off 3 sts at beg of next 6 (6, 6) rows.

Bind off.

Star Chart

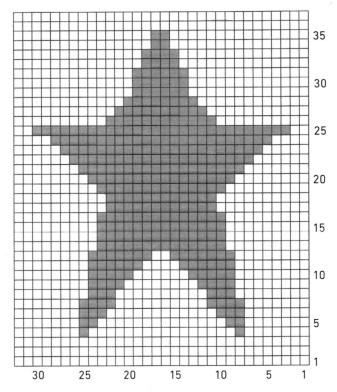

Finishing

Set in sleeves. Weave in ends. Block. Sew sleeve seams and body seams.

George R. R. Martin

DIRE WOLF

By Noel Anderson-Corwin

Who doesn't want their own cute and cuddly dire wolf to protect them from the dark things that lurk in the woods? This little one is a perfect size plushie and being cuddled by Mr. George R. R. Martin, creator of *Game of Thrones*!

Knit it in the round starting at the tail and ending at the nose. Legs are worked separately, also in the round, then joined using two I-cords to create moveable limbs for a frolicking, leaping, or lounging beast! Stuff the wolf as you knit. The short-row shaping technique is used extensively to create the wolf's curves, so be sure to hide all the wraps as you work for a smooth, clean finish!

MATERIALS

Superwash DK by Knit Picks, (100% superwash merino wool),
   3½ ounce (100g) balls, each approx. 246 yards (224m)
   2 balls in Bare (A)
Aloft by Knit Picks (75% super kid mohair, 25% silk),
   .88 ounce (25g) balls, each approx. 246 yards (224m)
   1 ball in Silver (B)
   1 ball in Carbon (C)
Swish DK by Knit Picks (100% Superwash Merino Wool),
   1.76 ounce (50g) balls, each approx. 123 yards (112m)
   1 ball in Coal (D)
Set of size 5 (3.75mm) double-pointed needles
Stitch marker
Polyester fiberfill
Tapestry needle

DIFFICULTY LEVEL:
Medium

SIZES: One size

GAUGE

Gauge is not essential for this project.

DIRE WOLF

Tail, Body, and Head

With A and B held together, cast on 3 sts. Divide over 3 needles, pm, and join, being careful not to twist the sts.

Rounds 1–2: Knit.

Round 3: K1, M1R, k1, M1L, k1—5 sts.

Rounds 4–5: Knit.

Round 6: K1, M1R, k3, M1L, k1—7 sts.

Rounds 7–8: Knit.

Round 9: K1, M1R, k5, M1L, k1—9 sts.

Rounds 10–11: Knit.

Round 12: K2, M1L, k5, M1R, k2—11 sts.

Round 13: Knit.

Round 14: K2, M1L, k7, M1R, k2—13 sts.

Round 15: Knit.

Round 16: K2, M1L, k9, M1R, k2—15 sts

Round 17: Knit.

Round 18: K2, M1L, k11, M1R, k2—17 sts.

Round 19: Knit.

Round 20: K2, M1L, k13, M1R, k2—19 sts.

Rounds 21–28: Knit.

Round 29: K16, w&t, p13, w&t, k11, w&t, p9, w&t, k14.

Round 30: Knit.

Round 31: K7, M1L, k5, M1R, k7—21 sts.

Round 32: Knit.

Round 33: K7, M1L, k7, M1R, k7—23 sts.

Rounds 34–37: Knit.

Round 38: K20, w&t, p17, w&t, k13, w&t, p9, w&t, k16.

Rounds 39–44: Knit.

Round 45: K8, k2tog, k3, ssk, k8—21 sts.

Round 46: Knit.

Round 47: K7, k2tog, k3, ssk, k7—19 sts.

Round 48: K6, w&t, p12, w&t, k10, w&t, p8, w&t, k23.

Round 49: Knit.

Round 50: K2, sssk, k9, k3tog, k2—15 sts.

Round 51: K10, w&t, p5, w&t, k10.

Round 52: K11, [turn, p7, turn, k7] four times, pick up 7 sts, k2tog, k2.

Round 53: K2, ssk, pick up 7 sts, k2tog, k3, ssk, k10.

Round 54: K10, M1L, k5, M1R, k10—27 sts.

Round 55: K4, M1R, k5, M1L, k9, M1R, k5, M1L, k4—31 sts.

Round 56: Knit.

Round 57: K12, M1L, k7, M1R, k3, w&t, p15, w&t, k4, M1L, k7, M1R, k13—35 sts.

Round 58: Knit.

Round 59: K3, M1R, k3, w&t, p10, M1R, p3, w&t, k44.

Round 60: Knit.

Round 61: K8, w&t, p16, w&t, k45.

Round 62: K11, yo, ssk, k11, k2tog, yo, k11—37 sts.

Rounds 63–68: Knit.

Round 69: K15, M1L, k7, M1R, k15—39 sts.

Rounds 70–71: Knit.

Round 72: K16, M1L, k7, M1R, k16—41 sts.

Rounds 73–74: Knit.

Round 75: K17, M1L, k7, M1R, k17—43 sts.

Rounds 76–77: Knit.

Round 78: K18, M1L, k7, M1R, k18—45 sts.

Round 79: Knit.

Round 80: K19, M1L, k7, M1R, k19—47 sts.

Round 81: Knit.

Round 82: K4, ssk, k14, M1L, k7, M1R, k14, k2tog, k4.

Rounds 83–85: Knit.

Round 86: K4, ssk, k14, M1L, k7, M1R, k14, k2tog, k4.

Rounds 87–91: Knit.

Round 92: K20, M1L, k7, M1R, k20—49 sts.

Round 93: K42, w&t, p35, w&t, k14, M1L, k7, M1R, k11, w&t, p31, w&t, k26, w&t, p21, w&t, k36.

Round 94: K4, M1R, k21, k2tog, k5, ssk, k21, M1L, k4.

Round 95: K48, w&t, p37, w&t, k30, w&t, p23, w&t, k7, k2tog, k5, ssk, k25.

Round 96: Knit.

Round 97: K4, M1R, k18, M1L, k7, M1R, k18, M1L, k4.

Round 98: K18, yo, k19, yo, k18.

Round 99: K4, M1R, k42, w&t, p35, w&t, k30, w&t, p25, w&t, k37, M1L, k4—57 sts.

Round 100: Knit.

Round 101: K4, M1R, k49, M1L, k4—59 sts.

Round 102: K25, k2tog, k5, ssk, k25—57 sts.

Round 103: Knit.

Round 104: K24, k2tog, k5, ssk, k24—55 sts.

Round 105: K2, sssk, k45, k3tog, k2—51 sts.

Rounds 106–107: Knit.

Round 108: K17, ssk, k2, w&t, p37, p2tog, p2, w&t, k35, w&t, p30, w&t, k26, w&t, p22, w&t, k60.

Round 109: K20, k2tog, k5, ssk, k20—47 sts.

Round 110: Knit.

Round 111: K18, w&t, p36, w&t, k33, w&t, p30, w&t, k27, w&t, p24, w&t, k21, w&t, p17, w&t, k56.

Round 112: K2, ssk, k39, k2tog, k2—45 sts.

Rounds 113–114: Knit.

Round 115: K2, ssk, k12, w&t, p17, p2tog, p12, w&t, k17, ssk, k35, k2tog, k2.

Round 116: Knit.

Round 117: K2, ssk, k33, k2tog, k2—39 sts.

Round 118: K15, w&t, p30, w&t, k27, w&t, p24, w&t, k8, k2tog, k4, ssk, k5, w&t, p16, w&t, k4, k2tog, k4, ssk, k32.

Round 119: Knit.

Round 120: K6, w&t, p12, w&t, k10, w&t, p8, w&t, k39.

Round 121: K2, sssk, k25, k3tog, k2—31 sts.

Round 122: Knit.

Round 123: K2, ssk, k8, ssk, k3, k2tog, k8, k2tog, k2—27 sts.

Round 124: Knit.

Round 125: K2, ssk, k7, ssk, k1, k2tog, k7, k2tog, k2—23 sts.

Round 126: Knit.

Round 127: K2, ssk, k15, k2tog, k2—21 sts.

Round 128: Knit.

Round 129: K2, ssk, k4, k2tog, k1, ssk, k4, k2tog, k2—17 sts.

Round 130: Knit.

Round 131: K2, ssk, k2, k2tog, k1, ssk, k2, k2tog, k2—13 sts.

Round 132: Knit.

Round 133: K1, k2tog, k7, ssk, k1—11 sts.

Round 134: Knit.

Round 135: K4, sl2tog, k1, psso, k1. turn, p3. Turn, sl2tog, k1, psso.

Cut yarn and pull through the remaining loop, 6 sts remain—slide these onto one needle, change to D to work Nose.

Nose

Row 1 (WS): Purl.

Row 2: K2tog, k2, ssk—4 sts.

Row 3: Purl.

Row 4: K2tog, ssk—2 sts.

Row 5: Purl.

Row 6: Knit.

Bind off, leaving a long tail for sewing. Sew Nose over small opening of the mouth using the tail.

Ears

Right Ear

With A and B held together, cast on 12 sts. Divide over 3 needles, pm, and join, being careful not to twist the sts.

Rounds 1–2: K1, p4, k7.

Round 3: K1, p3, k2tog, ssk, k4—10 sts.

Round 4: K1, p3, k6.

Round 5: K1, p2, k2tog, ssk, k3—8 sts.

Round 6: K1, p1, k2tog, ssk, k2—6 sts.

Round 7: K1, k2tog, k3—5 sts.

Round 8: Ssk, sssk—2 sts.

Cut yarn, draw through remaining sts, pull tight, and secure.

Left Ear

With A and B held together, cast on 12 sts. Divide over 3 needles, pm, and join, being careful not to twist the sts.

Rounds 1–2: K1, p4, k7.

Round 3: Ssk, p3, k5, k2tog—10 sts.

Round 4: K1, p3, k6.

Round 5: Ssk, p2, k4, k2tog—8 sts.

Round 6: Ssk, p1, k3, k2tog—6 sts.

Round 7: Ssk, k4—5 sts.

Round 8: K2tog, k3tog—2 sts.

Cut yarn, draw through remaining sts, pull tight, and secure.

Right Front Leg

With A and C held together, cast on 5 sts. Do not join.

Row 1: Purl.

Row 2: Knit.

Row 3: Purl.

Row 4: K1, M1L, k3, M1R, k1—7 sts.

With RS facing, pick up and knit 8 sts as follows: Using a second needle, pick up and knit 3 sts along the right edge and 1 st along cast-on edge; using a third needle, pick up and knit 1 st along the cast-on edge and 3 sts along the left edge. Pm and join for working in the round—15 sts.

Rounds 1–2: Knit.

Round 3: K1, M1R, k5, M1L, k9—17 sts.

Round 4: Knit.

Round 5: K2, M1R, k5, M1L, k10—19 sts.

Rounds 6–9: Knit.

Round 10: K1, w&t, p10, w&t, k8, w&t, p6, w&t, k26.

Round 11: Knit.

Round 12: K1, ssk, k5, k2tog, k9—17 sts.

Round 13: K9, w&t, p3, w&t, k1, M1R, k1, M1L, w&t, p3, w&t, k2tog, ssk, k8.

Round 14: K1, w&t, p10, w&t, k8, w&t, p6, w&t, k24.

Round 15: Knit.

Round 16: K7, k2tog, k8—16 sts.

Rounds 17–26: Knit.

Round 27: K1, M1R, k6, M1L, k9—18 sts.

Rounds 28–32: Knit.

Round 33: K2, M1R, k6, M1L, k10—20 sts.

Rounds 34–37: Knit.

Round 38: K3, M1R, k6, M1L, k11—22 sts.

Rounds 39–41: Knit.

Round 42: K3, ssk, k4, k2tog, k4, M1R, k6, M1L, k1.

Round 43: Knit.

Round 44: K3, ssk, k2, k2tog, k3, w&t, p10, w&t, k3, ssk, k2tog, k4 (hiding wrap), M1R, k2, M1R, k4, M1L, k2, M1L, k1.

Round 45: Knit.

Round 46: K2, k2tog, ssk, k4, M1R, k2, w&t, p14, M1R, p1, w&t, k6, k2tog, ssk, k4, yo, k2tog, k11.

Round 47: K2tog, ssk, k6, k2tog, ssk, k6—16 sts.

Round 48: K2tog, ssk, k3, k3tog, sssk, k3—10 sts.

Round 49: K2tog, ssk, k3tog, sssk—4 sts.

Cut yarn, draw through remaining sts, pull tight, and secure.

Left Front Leg

With A and C held together, cast on 5 sts. Do not join.

Row 1: Purl.

Row 2: Knit.

Row 3: Purl.

Row 4: K1, M1L, k3, M1R, k1—7 sts. With RS facing, pick up and knit 8 sts as follows: Using a second needle, pick up and knit 3 sts along the side and 1 st along the top; using a third needle, pick up and knit 1 st along the top and 3 sts along the side. Pm and join for working in the round—15 sts.

Rounds 1–12: Work as for Right Front Leg.

Round 13: K3, w&t, p3, w&t, k1, M1R, k1, M1L, w&t, p3, w&t, k2tog, ssk, k14.

Round 14: K1, w&t, p10, w&t, k8, w&t, p6, w&t, k24.

Round 15: Knit.

Round 16: Ssk, k15—16 sts.

Rounds 17–26: Knit.

Round 27: K1, M1R, k6, M1L, k9—18 sts.

Rounds 28–32: Knit.

Round 33: K2, M1R, k6, M1L, k10—20 sts.

Rounds 34–37: Knit.

Round 38: K3, M1R, k6, M1L, k11—22 sts.

Rounds 39–41: Knit.

Round 42: K3, ssk, k4, k2tog, k4, M1R, k6, M1L, k1.

Round 43: Knit.

Round 44: K3, ssk, k2, k2tog, k3, w&t, p10, w&t, k3, ssk, k2tog, k4 (hiding wrap), M1R, k2, M1R, k4, M1L, k2, M1L, k1.

Round 45: Knit.

Round 46: K2, k2tog, ssk, k4, M1R, k2, w&t, p14, M1R, p1, w&t, k2, yo, ssk, k2, k2tog, ssk, k17.

Round 47: K2tog, ssk, k6, k2tog, ssk, k6—16 sts.

Round 48: K2tog, ssk, k3, k3tog, sssk, k3—10 sts.

Round 49: K2tog, ssk, k3tog, sssk—4 sts. Cut yarn, draw through remaining sts, pull tight, and secure.

With A and C held together, pick up and knit 5 sts around eyelet (from round 46) on the Left Front Leg. Work these 5 sts as an I-cord for 6 rows. Bind off, leaving a 12" tail.

Right Rear Leg

With A and C held together, cast on 5 sts. Do not join.

Row 1: Purl.

Row 2: Knit.

Row 3: Purl.

Row 4: K1, M1L, k3, M1R, k1—7 sts. With RS facing, pick up and knit 8 sts as follows: Using a second needle, pick up and knit 3 sts along the side and 1 st along the top; using a third needle, pick up and knit 1 st along the top and 3 sts along the side. Pm and join for working in the round—15 sts.

Rounds 1–2: Knit.

Round 3: K1, M1R, k5, M1L, k9—17 sts.

Round 4: Knit.

Round 5: K2, M1R, k5, M1L, k10—19 sts.

Rounds 6–9: Knit.

Round 10: K1, w&t, p10, w&t, k8, w&t, p6, w&t, k26.

Round 11: Knit.

Round 12: K1, ssk, k5, k2tog, k9—17 sts.

Rounds 13–21: Knit.

Round 22: K2tog, k5, ssk, k8—15 sts.

Round 23: Knit.

Round 24: K10, w&t, p13, w&t, k11, w&t, p9, w&t, k8, w&t, p7, w&t, ssk, k3, k2tog, k3, M1R, k2, M1L, k3.

Round 25: Knit.

Round 26: Ssk, k1, k2tog, k4, M1R, w&t, p12, M1R, w&t, k10, w&t, p7, w&t, k17.

Round 27: Knit.

Round 28: K8, M1R, k2, M1L, k5—17 sts.

Round 29: Knit.

Round 30: K9, M1R, k2, M1L, k6—19 sts.

Round 31: K18, w&t, p14, w&t, k6, M1R, k2, M1L, k5, w&t, p14, w&t, k6, M1R, k2, M1L, k5, w&t, p14, w&t, k6, M1R, k2, M1L, k5, w&t, p14, w&t, k6, M1R, k2, M1L, k10.

Round 32: Knit.

Round 33: K14, M1R, k2, M1L, k11—29 sts.

Round 34: K3, M1L, k26, M1R—31 sts.

Round 35: K26, w&t, p18, w&t, k8, M1R, k2, M1L, k6, w&t, p16, w&t, k23.

Rounds 36–38: Knit.

Round 39: K3, M1L, k25, w&t, p20, w&t, k25, M1R.

Round 40: Knit.

Round 41: K3, ssk, k11, k2tog, k2, ssk, k11, k2tog—31 sts.

Round 42: K3, ssk, k5, yo, k3, k3tog, k2, ssk, k9, k2tog—27 sts.

Round 43: K3, ssk, k7, k2tog, k2, ssk, k7, k2tog—23 sts.

Round 44: K3, ssk, k5, k2tog, k2, ssk, k5, k2tog—19 sts.

Round 45: K3, ssk, k3, k2tog, k2, ssk, k3, k2tog—15 sts.

Round 46: K3, ssk, k1, k2tog, k2, ssk, k1, k2tog—11 sts.

Round 47: Sl2tog, k1, psso, k3tog, k2, sssk—5 sts.

Cut yarn, draw through remaining sts, pull tight, and secure.

Left Rear Leg

With A and C held together, cast on 5 sts. Do not join.

Row 1: Purl.

Row 2: Knit.

Row 3: Purl.

Row 4: K1, M1L, k3, M1R, k1—7 sts.

With RS facing, pick up and knit 8 sts as follows: Using a second needle, pick up and knit 3 sts along the side and 1 st along the top; using a third needle, pick up and knit 1 st along the top and 3 sts along the side. Pm and join for working in the round—15 sts.

Rounds 1–41: Work as for Right Rear Leg.

Round 42: K3, k9, k2tog, k2, sssk, k3, yo, k5, k2tog—27 sts.

Round 43: K3, ssk, k7, k2tog, k2, ssk, k7, k2tog—23 sts.

Round 44: K3, ssk, k5, k2tog, k2, ssk, k5, k2tog—19 sts.

Round 45: K3, ssk, k3, k2tog, k2, ssk, k3, k2tog—15 sts.

Round 46: K3, ssk, k1, k2tog, k2, ssk, k1, k2tog—11 sts.

Round 47: Sl2tog, k1, psso, k3tog, k2, sssk—5 sts.

Cut yarn, draw through remaining sts, pull tight, and secure.

With A and C held together, pick up and knit 5 sts around eyelet (from round 41) on the Left Back Leg. Work these 5 sts as an I-cord for 4 rows. Bind off, leaving a 12" tail.

Finishing

Attach the ears to the top of the Dire Wolf's head. With D, embroider eyes.

Attach Front Legs to Body: With yarn needle, pull the I-cord on the Left Front Leg through both eyelets on the front end of the Dire Wolf's body and attach the cord to the Right Front Leg where the eyelet is to ensure both legs are even.

Attach Back Legs to Body: With yarn needle, pull the I-cord on the Left Back Leg through both eyelets on the back end of the Dire Wolf's body and attach the cord to the Right Back Leg where the eyelet is to ensure both legs are even.

Weave in ends.

Miracle Laurie

Dragon Rider Shrug

By Joan of Dark

Dragons appear in all sorts of sci-fi and fantasy fiction. This shrug was designed with the dragon rider or trainer in mind. Knit in one long piece and seamed on the arms, it features a built-in thumbhole to help it stay in place no matter how high you choose to fly! The garter stitch around the cable pattern is nice and stretchy, so if your arms get muscular from trying to steer a fire-breathing beast around, the shrug will still fit!

While this pattern is listed with a difficulty level of Medium due to the cable, increasing, and decreasing, the beginner shouldn't be scared to give it a try! After all, you need some bravery to handle a dragon, so let that bravery cross over into your knitting!

MATERIALS

Swish Worsted by Knit Picks (100% superwash merino wool),
    1¾ ounce (50g) balls, each approx. 110 yards (100m)
    4 (5, 5, 6) balls in Lava Heather
One US size 7 (4.5mm) circular needle, 16" long
    (or set of straight needles, if you prefer)
Cable needle
Two stitch markers
Tapestry needle

GAUGE

19 sts and 21 rows = 4" (10cm) in garter st

DIFFICULTY LEVEL:
Medium

SIZES: Small (Medium, Large, Extra Large)

MEASUREMENTS TO FIT

10–13" (13–15, 15–17, 17–19) upper arm
15–16" (16–17, 17–19, 19–22) back

NOTES ABOUT SIZING

This shrug comes in small, medium, large, and extra-large. However, a person with extra-large arms can still be petite when it comes to back width! If your arms match the width for the extra-large size, but you're on the short side with a smaller back, it might behoove you to follow the larger size for increasing and decreasing, but use the smaller size for how many inches to work the cable without increases across the back.

Also, it should be noted that this pattern is extremely easy to customize when it comes to sizes! Work the increases and decreases on cable rows 1 and 5 if you need a larger size without so much length! Dragon riders come in all shapes and sizes!

SPECIAL ABBREVIATIONS

C6B: Slip 3 sts to cable needle and hold in back, k3, k3 from cable needle.
C6F: Slip 3 sts to cable needle and hold in front, k3, k3 from cable needle.

Cable Pattern

Row 1 (RS): Knit to marker, sm, knit to second marker, sm, knit to end.
Row 2: Knit to marker, sm, purl to second marker, sm, knit to end.
Row 3: Knit to marker, sm, [C6B] 3 times, sm, knit to end.
Row 4: Repeat row 2.
Row 5: Repeat row 1.
Row 6: Repeat row 2.
Row 7: Knit to marker, sm, k3, [C6F] two times, k3, sm, knit to end.
Row 8: Repeat row 2.
Repeat rows 1–8 for pattern.

SHRUG

First Sleeve

Cast on 40 (48, 54, 58) sts.
Rows 1–6: Knit.
Row 7: K11 (15, 18, 20), pm, k18, pm, knit to end.
Row 8: Knit to second marker, sm, k3, bind off 5 (6, 6, 6) sts, knit to end.
Row 9 (RS): Knit to bound off sts, cast on 5 (6, 6, 6) sts, knit to end.
Rows 10–15: Work rows 3–8 of cable pattern.
Row 16: Knit to 2 sts before marker, kf&b, k1, sm, knit to second marker, sm, k1, kf&b, knit to end of row—42 (50, 56, 60) sts.

Rows 17–23: Work rows 2–8 of cable pattern.

Repeat last 8 rows 20 (20, 21, 22) more times—82 (90, 98, 104) sts.

Back

Continue working in Cable Pattern until piece measures 38" (40, 41, 42).

Second Sleeve

Begin decrease rows:

Row 1: Knit to 3 sts before marker, ssk, k1, sm, knit to second marker, sm, k1, k2tog, knit to end—80 (88, 96, 102) sts.

Work rows 2–8 of Cable Pattern.

Repeat last 8 rows until 40 (48, 54, 58) sts remain.

Work rows 1–7 of Cable Pattern.

Next Row (WS): Knit to second marker, sm, k3, bind off 5 (6, 6, 6) sts, knit to end.

Next Row: Knit to bound off sts, cast on 5 (6, 6, 6) sts, knit to end.

Knit 6 rows.

Bind off.

Finishing

Seam up 21" (22, 22½, 23) on each side for arms (or desired arm length).

Leave back (center portion) open.

Weave in ends. Block lightly.

Dragon Rider Schematic

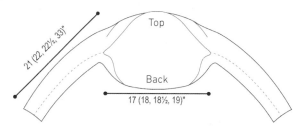

21 (22, 22½, 33)"

Top

Back

17 (18, 18½, 19)"

Roman Dirge

Broken Blade Hooded Sweater

By Joan of Dark

This hooded sweater, inspired by the Kelly McCullough's Fallen Blade series, is a great knit for those looking to tackle their first sweater! Big and chunky, it knits up quickly and is perfectly warm and cozy. With its hood and dark color, it's great for lurking around outside as well!

MATERIALS

Wool Ease Chunky by Lion Brand (80% acrylic, 20% wool),
   5 ounce (140g) skeins, each approx. 153 yards (139m)
   6 (6, 7) skeins in True Black
Size 10½ (6.5mm) circular needles, 12" and 16" long
Stitch markers
Stitch holders
Tapestry needle
Note: Body is not worked in the round; circular needle
   suggested for ease.

DIFFICULTY LEVEL: Medium

SIZES: Small (Medium, Large)

TO FIT: 34–36" (38–40, 42–44) chest

GAUGE

12 sts and 24 rows = 4" (10cm) in garter st

SWEATER

Back

Cast on 71 (79, 87) sts using longer circular needle.
Work in garter st (knit every row) for 18½" (19, 19½).

Bind off 12 (14, 16) sts at beg of next two rows—47 (51, 55) sts.

Work garter st for 9" (9½, 10).

Bind off 11 (13, 15) sts at beg of next two rows.

Place remaining 25 (25, 25) sts on stitch holder.

Front

Work same as back.

Sew shoulder seams.

Neck and Hood

Slip sts from holders to shorter circular needle—50 sts.

Round 1: Join yarn at left neck edge (as sweater is facing you), pm, and knit around.

Round 2: Purl.

Round 3: Knit, increasing 10 sts evenly around—60 sts.

Round 4: Purl.

Rounds 5–22: Continue in circular garter st as set.

Round 23: Bind off 30 sts for front neck, leaving remaining 30 sts on needles.

Begin Hood

Row 1: Knit to end of row, pick up and knit 1 st at neck edge—31 sts.

Row 2: Knit to end of row, pick up and knit 1 st at neck edge—32 sts.

Row 3: Knit, increasing 10 sts evenly across—42 sts.

Row 4: Knit.

Row 5: K14, pm, k14, pm, knit to end.

Row 6: Knit.

Row 7: Knit to marker, M1, sl marker, knit to marker, sl marker, M1, knit to end—2 sts increased.

Row 8: Knit.

Repeat Rows 7 and 8 27 more times—98 sts. Work even in garter st for an additional 2" (2½, 3). *Note:* Leave your stitch markers in. You'll need them for the decrease section. Begin decrease rows:

Row 1: Knit to 2 sts before marker, k2tog, sm, knit to second marker, sm, ssk, knit to end. 2 sts decreased.

Row 2: Knit.

Broken Blade

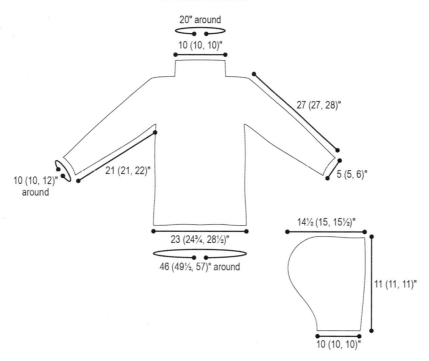

20" around

10 (10, 10)"

27 (27, 28)"

10 (10, 12)"
around

21 (21, 22)"

5 (5, 6)"

23 (24¾, 28½)"

46 (49½, 57)" around

14½ (15, 15½)"

11 (11, 11)"

10 (10, 10)"

Repeat these two rows 10 times—78 sts.
Bind off.
Fold hood in half vertically, and with RS facing, seam top edge.

Sleeves

Cast on 33 (33, 37) sts.
Work in garter st for 3" (3, 3½).
Increase 1 st at beg and end of each row every sixth row 11 (11, 13) times—55 (55, 63) sts.
Work even in garter st until sleeve measures 21" (21, 22) from cast on edge.

Shape Cap

Bind off 6 sts at beg of next two rows—43 (43, 51) sts.
Decrease 1 st at each side every fourth row until 9 (9, 11) sts remain.
Place remaining sts on holder.

Finishing

Set in Sleeves. Sew side and sleeve seams.
Weave in ends.
Block, wear when sneaking around in the shadows. Or while curling up with a good book. Whichever floats your boat.

Roman Dirge

Bunnicula

By Claire Reagan

Who can resist a vampire when it's so darn adorable? This cute little bunny is based off the James Howe series Bunnicula! Very easy to knit up for the intermediate knitter or the knitter looking to dive into toys for the first time. Head and body are knit together, with the legs and ears knit separately. Bonus carrot pattern included—but looks like bunny already sucked it dry!

MATERIALS

Vanna's Choice by Lion Brand (100% premium acrylic),
   3½ ounce (100g) skeins, each approx. 170 yards (155m)
   2 skeins in White (A)
   1 skein in Black (B)
   1 skein in Pink (C)
One pair US size 6 (4mm) straight needles
Stitch holder
Polyester fiberfill
Two red buttons (for eyes)
Tapestry needle
Large pom-pom maker

DIFFICULTY LEVEL:
Medium

SIZES: One size

GAUGE

22 sts and 30 rows = 4" (10cm) in St st

SPECIAL ABBREVIATIONS

M1L: Make 1 left: Lift strand between sts front to back and knit into the back of it.

ssp: Slip 2 sts knitwise, one at a time. Place back on left needle, purl together through back loops.

BUNNY

Body

With A, cast on 10 sts.

Row 1 and all odd rows to row 13: Purl.

Row 2: *K1, M1L; repeat from * to last st, k1—19 sts.

Row 4: Repeat row 2—37 sts.

Row 6: *K2, M1L; repeat from * to last st, k1—55 sts.

Row 8: *K3, M1L; repeat from * to last st, k1—73 sts.

Row 10: Knit.

Row 12: *K4, M1L; repeat from * 17 times, knit to end—90 sts.

Row 13: Purl.

From here, you will work the Back chart in the center of the piece, joining colors B and A as you need them. It's worked using the Intarsia method—you may find that small bobbins will make it easier.

Row 14: With A, k28, pm for start of chart, work Body chart across next 24 sts, pm, with A k to end of row.

Chart is set. Continue in st st until chart row 31 is complete

Row 32: With A, k14, ssk, k10, k2tog, work in patt as set to last 28 sts, ssk, k10, k2tog, k14—86 sts.

Row 33 and all following WS rows: Work even in patt as set.

Row 34: With A, k14, ssk, k8, k2tog, work in patt as set to last 26 sts, ssk, k8, k2tog, k14—82 sts.

Row 36: With A, k14, ssk, k6, k2tog, work in patt as set to last 24 sts, ssk, k6, k2tog, k14—78 sts.

Row 38: With A, k14, ssk, k4, k2tog, work in patt as set to last 22 sts, ssk, k4, k2tog, k14—74 sts.

Row 40: With A, k14, ssk, k2, k2tog, work in patt as set to last 20 sts, ssk, k2, k2tog, k14—70 sts.

Row 42: With A, k14, ssk, k2tog, work in patt as set to last 18 sts, ssk, k2tog, k14—66 sts.

Row 44: With A, k14, k2tog, work in patt as set to last 16 sts, k2tog, k14—64 sts.

Row 46: With A, k13, k2tog, work in patt as set to last 15 sts, k2tog, k13—62 sts.

Row 48: With A, k12, k2tog, work in patt as set to last 14 sts, k2tog, k12—60 sts.

Row 50: With A, k11, k2tog, work in patt as set to last 13 sts, k2tog, k11—58 sts.

Row 52: With A, k10, k2tog, work in patt as

set to last 12 sts, k2tog, k10—56 sts.

Row 54: With A, k9, k2tog, work in patt as set to last 11 sts, k2tog, k9—54 sts.

Row 56: With A, k8, k2tog, work in patt as set to last 10 sts k2tog, k8—52 sts.

Row 58: With A, k7, k2tog, work in patt as set to last 9 sts, k2tog, k7—50 sts.

Row 60: With A, k6, k2tog, work in patt as set to last 8 sts, k2tog, k6—48 sts.

Row 62: With A, k5, k2tog, work in patt as set to last 7 sts, k2tog, k5—46 sts.

Row 64: With A, k4, k2tog, work in patt as set to last 6 sts, k2tog, k4—44 sts.

Remove chart markers.

Head

Row 66: With A, [k2tog] nine times; with B, k8; with A, [k2tog] nine times—26 sts.

Row 67: With A, p1, [p2tog] three times, p2; with B, p8; with A, p2, [p2tog] three times, p1—20 sts.

Row 68: ★K1, M1L; repeat from ★ 19 times, kf&b, keeping in color pattern (12 sts A, 16 sts B, 12 sts A)—40 sts.

Row 69: With A, p12; with B, p16; with A, p12.

Row 70: ★K2, M1L; repeat from ★ to last st, kfb, keeping in color pattern, (18 sts A, 24 sts B, 18 sts A)—60 sts.

Row 71: With A, p18; pm for start of chart, work Head chart across next 24 sts, pm for end of chart, with A, p18.

Work even as set until Chart Row 81 is complete. As you decrease away the side stitches, continue to work Head chart as set.

Row 82: With A, k5, ssk, k11, ssk, work as set to last 20 st, k2tog, k11, k2tog, k5— 56 sts.

Row 83, 85, 87: Work even in patt as set.

Row 84: With A, k5, ssk, k10, ssk, work as set to last 19 sts, k2tog, k10, k2tog, k5—52 sts.

Row 86: With A, k5, ssk, k9, ssk, work as set to last 18 sts, k2tog, k9, k2tog, k5—48 sts.

Row 88: With A, k5, ssk, k8, ssk, work as set to last 17 sts, k2tog, k8, k2tog, k5—44 sts. Chart is complete.

Row 89: With A, p21; with B, p2tog; with A, p21—43 sts.

Row 90: With A, k5, ssk, k7, ssk, k5; with B, k1; with A, k5, k2tog, k7, k2tog, k5—39 sts. Cut B.

Row 91: With A, purl.

Row 92: With A, k5, ssk, k6, ssk, k9, k2tog, k6, k2tog, k5—35 sts.

Row 93 and all remaining odd rows: Purl.

Row 94: K5, ssk, k5, ssk, k7, k2tog, k5, k2tog, k5—31 sts.

Row 96: K5, ssk, k4, ssk, k5, k2tog, k4, k2tog, k5—27 sts.

Row 98: Knit.

Row 100: K2tog to last st, k1—14 sts.

Row 102: K2tog across—7 sts.

Cut yarn, draw through remaining sts, pull tight, and secure.

Sew Head together (from nose to neck)

using mattress stitch and stuff to desired firmness, weaving in ends prior to stuffing. Continue to sew Body together, stuffing as work progresses. At the end of the seam (bunny bottom), gather the cast-on edge, pull tight, and secure.

Front Legs (make 2)

With A, cast on 5 sts.

Row 1 and all odd rows: Purl.

Row 2: *K1, M1L; repeat from * to last st, k1—9 sts.

Row 4: Repeat row 2—17 sts.

Rows 5–27: Work in St st.

Row 28: K2tog to last st, k1—9 sts.

Row 30: K2tog to last st, k1—5 sts.

Cut yarn, draw through remaining sts, pull tight, and secure.

Weave in ends prior to stuffing. Sew seam using mattress stitch and stuff to desired firmness. Sew Front Legs in place on Body.

Rear Legs (make 2)

With A, cast on 50 sts.

Rows 1–9: Beginning with a purl row, work in St st.

Row 10: [K2tog] three times, knit to end—47 sts.

Row 11: [P2tog] three times, purl to end—44 sts.

Rows 12–13: Repeat rows 10 and 11 once—38 sts.

Row 14: Bind off 9 sts, knit to end—29 sts.

Row 15: Bind off 9 sts, purl to end—20 sts.

Row 16: Knit.

Row 17: P20, cast on 3 sts—23 sts.

Row 18: K23, cast on 3 sts—26 sts.

Row 19: P26, cast on 3 sts—29 sts.

Row 20: K29, cast on 3 sts—32 sts.

Row 21–39 and all odd rows: Purl.

Row 22: K1, M1L, k30, M1L, k1—34 sts.

Row 24: K1, M1L, k32, M1L, k1—36 sts.

Row 26: K1, M1L, k34, M1L, k1—38 sts.

Row 28: K1, M1L, k36, M1L, k1—40 sts.

Rows 29–33: Work in St st.

Row 34: K1, ssk, knit to last 3 sts, k2tog, k1—38 sts.

Row 36: K1, ssk, knit to last 3 sts, k2tog, k1—36 sts.

Row 38: K1, ssk, knit to last 3 sts, k2tog, k1—34 sts.

Row 40: K1, ssk, k12, k2tog (15 sts on right needle), place remaining 17 sts on holder. Continue on 15 sts only.

Row 41: P1, p2tog, purl to last 3 sts, ssp, p1—2 sts decreased.

Row 42: K1, ssk, knit to last 3 sts, k2tog, k1—2 sts decreased.

Rows 43–45: Repeat rows 41 and 42 and then row 41 once more—5 sts.

Bind off.

Return 17 held sts on needle.

Row 1: K1, ssk, knit to last 3 sts, k2tog, k1—15 sts.

Row 2: P1, p2tog, purl to last 3 sts, ssp, p1—13 sts.

Rows 3–6: Repeat rows 1 and 2 twice—5 sts.

Bind off.

Fold foot in half, matching the sides, and sew around the outer edge using mattress stitch. Sew the seam using mattress stitch and stuff to desired firmness. Sew Back Legs in place on Body.

Ears (make 2 with B and 2 with C)

Cast on 10 sts.

Rows 1–4: Work in St st, beg and ending with RS row.

Row 5: K2, M1L, knit to last 2 sts, M1L, k2—2 sts increased.

Row 6: Purl.

Row 7: Knit.

Row 8: Purl.

Rows 9–24: Repeat rows 5–8 four more times—20 sts.

Rows 25–30: Work in St st.

Row 31: K1, ssk, knit to last 3 sts, k2tog, k1—2 sts decreased.

Row 32: Purl.

Rows 33–42: Repeat rows 31 and 32 five times more—8 sts.

Bind off.

Using mattress stitch, sew one B Ear to one C Ear. Repeat with remaining Ears. Sew in place on Head, smaller end at bottom.

Tail

With A, make a pom-pom using a scrap of cardboard or use pom-pom maker. Sew in place on Body.

Finishing

With C, embroider nose. With B, embroider mouth and fangs as shown. Sew buttons in place for eyes.

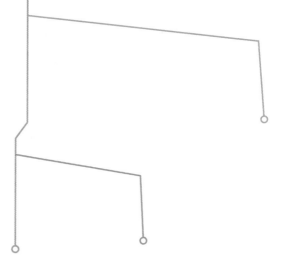

Head Chart

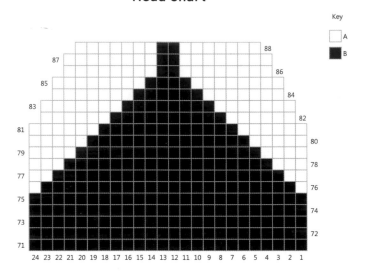

Back Chart

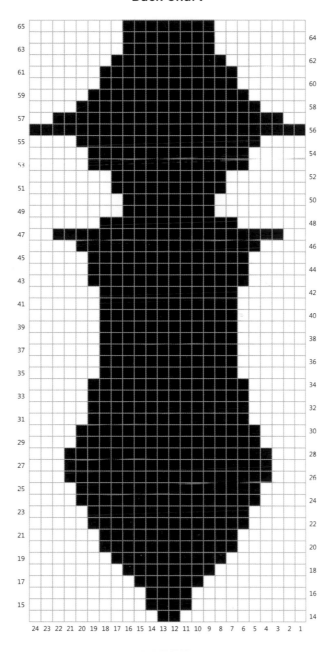

Peter Sagal

THE RUNNING DEAD HEADBAND AND HAT

By Emma Bull

How often has this happened to you? You're fleeing the neighborhood zombies. You reach home just ahead of the pack, charge up your front steps . . . and realize your house key was left behind in the jacket you squirmed out of to escape their clutches. You're locked out. The zombies eat your brains.

Ward off this annoying post-apocalyptic scenario by knitting and wearing this headband or hat with a secret inside pocket for your valuables. As long as you keep your head—literally speaking—you'll be fine.

Knit the crown of the hat version in a bright color to help search-and-rescue teams find you—or your remains! And since the stranded colorwork band is extra-thick and cozy, you'll be protected from frostbite or, er, bites, whether you're following Rule Number One, fetching supplies for Abel Township, or just trying to keep Carl in the house.

MATERIALS

For Headband

Swish Worsted by Knit Picks (100% superwash merino wool), 1¾ ounce (50g) balls, each approx. 110 yards (100m)

2 balls in Eggpant (A)

1 ball in Peapod (B)

DIFFICULTY LEVEL: Hard

SIZE: Medium

To Fit: 21–22" head circumference

NOTE ON SIZING: If needed, use a smaller or larger needle to adjust size.

For Hat

Swish Worsted by Knit Picks (100%
    superwash merino wool), 1¾ ounce (50g)
    balls, each approx. 110 yards (100m)
    2 balls in Black (A)
    1 ball in Peapod (B)
    1 ball in Orange (C)

For Both

Size 6 (4mm) circular needle, 16" long
Set of size 6 (4mm) double-pointed needles
Size 5 (3.75mm) circular needle, 16" long
Stitch marker
Two stitch markers
Tapestry needle

GAUGE

20½ sts and 32 rnds = 4" (10cm) in St st
    using smaller needle

Special Techniques
Fair Isle Tips

- You can hold both colors of yarn in your left hand or your right hand, or you can use one hand for each color. But make sure you keep the contrast color strand to the left side of the main color strand. Pretend they're the driver and passenger in a car, and the passenger doesn't know how to drive, so whatever you do, keep the passenger out of the driver's seat!

- When you switch from one color to the other, make sure the contrast color always passes under the main color.

- As you make stitches with one color, the unused color forms a strand across the back of the work called a "float." Keep this strand a little slack, so it doesn't prevent the finished fabric from stretching. Spacing your stitches out along the right-hand needle as you work will help keep your floats loose.

- When you work more than five or six stitches in a row of the contrast color, as on the zombies' arms or the runner's shoulders, you can keep the float of the main color from getting too long and floppy by twisting it with the working yarn halfway through the long set of stitches. Loop the floating yarn

Running Dead Chart

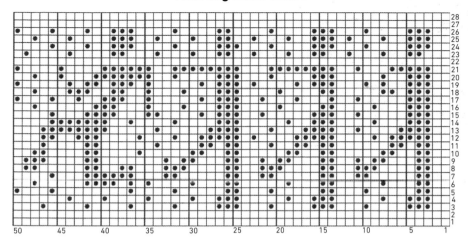

□ − A
● − B

over the top of the working yarn, then back under it to its original position. Remember, don't change drivers! Make sure you keep that shortened float slack, as you did the others.

HEADBAND

With larger circular needle and A, cast on 100 sts using long-tail cast-on. Pm and join, being careful not to twist the sts.

Switch to smaller needle.

Rounds 1–4: [K1, p1] seven times, knit to end.

Round 5: Knit.

Repeat round 5 until piece measures 3¾" from cast-on edge.

Switch to larger needle. Purl one round.

(This makes a nifty edge on the hem.) Begin chart, working blank squares in A and dotted squares in B.

When chart is complete, weave in ends. Once you complete the next step, you won't be able to get to the back of the work. Don't weave in your cast-on tail yet, though, because it will make it harder to find the edge of the first st.

Use removable stitch markers or safety pins to mark the first and last of the 14 ribbing sts at the cast-on edge. These are the two sides of the pocket opening. Fold the work at the row of purl stitches, WS together. The solid color section you knitted first is now on the inside, and your cast-on edge is the inside top, parallel to the sts on your needle.

The beginning-of-row marker on your needle and the marker for the first ribbing st should be side by side.

Join and Bind Off

Bind off the first 14 sts, alternating knit and purl as if it were a ribbed edge. This will reduce the edge's tendency to curl. Starting at the marker placed at the end of the pocket ribbing, examine the cast-on edge on the inside of the Headband. You'll see a line of sideways V shapes along the top. Use your right needle to pick up the leg of the V closest to the inside of the Headband and transfer it without twisting to the left needle.

Knit the picked-up st together with the next st on the left needle. Loosely bind off 1 st. Repeat that pick-up and knit with the next V in the cast-on edge and bind off again.

Continue picking up sts, knitting them together, and binding off loosely until all the sts are bound off.

Finishing

Weave in ends. Block.

HAT

Work as for Headband to just before Join and Bind Off section and continue as follows:

To Join

Knit 14. As described in the Headband section, pick up the first st of the cast-on edge after the ribbing with the tip of your right needle, transfer it without twisting to the left needle, and knit it together with the next st on the needle.

Continue to pick up sts from the cast-on edge and knit them together with the sts on the left needle until you reach the beginning-of-row marker. All the inside edge sts will be picked up except the 14 ribbing sts. Switch to C and knit 1 round.

Shape Crown

Note: Change to dpns when needed.

Round 1: [K3, k2tog] around—80 sts.

Round 2 and even rounds through 8: Knit.

Round 3: [K2, k2tog] around—60 sts.

Round 5: [K1, k2tog] around—40 sts.

Round 7: [K2tog] around—20 sts.

Round 9: [K2tog] around—10 sts.

Round 10: [K2tog] around—5 sts.

Cut yarn, draw through remaining sts, pull tight, and secure.

Finishing

Weave in ends. Block.

THE EVERYDAY GEEK

Don't think that "everyday" means boring! The Everyday Geek is a section for gamers, writers, and mystery solvers! "Geeks" aren't just limited to sci-fi and fantasy conventions. I personally have become a total fountain pen geek in the past year! (Did you know there are fountain pen conventions? How cool is that?) Lots of people consider themselves geeks about one thing or another. Are you a chess geek? Knit a scarf that pieces together to become a chessboard and a warm fashion statement! Love curling up on the couch to solve a good mystery? Knit an updated version of the classic Sherlock-inspired deerstalker! Gamer geek? How about knitting some awesome dice pillows? There are all sorts of ways to geek out! Hopefully the patterns in this section will inspire whatever sort of geek affection you have.

Neil Gaiman

Baker Street Hat

By Joan of Dark

This hat is a bit of a riff on the traditional deerstalker made famous by Sherlock Holmes. Though he was always pictured in a deerstalker, Sherlock most likely wouldn't have worn a hunting hat, as he was usually in the city. (Except, of course, in "Hound of the Baskervilles"!)

This hat, however, is great for the modern mystery solver. A nod to the deerstalker style, except in a more modern black and with much shorter brims. Easy to modify by removing a brim or the ear flaps, and perfectly warm to fend off the chill during those midnight chases through the city!

The body of the hat is knit in one piece with the brim and earflaps added on after. A great project for a knitter who likes to customize!

MATERIALS

Andes del Campo Heavy Worsted Weight by Knit Picks
    (100% Highland wool), 3½ ounce (100g) balls,
    each approx. 164 yards (149m)
    1 (2) ball(s) in Wellies Heather
Size 8 (5mm) circular needle, 16" long
Set of size 8 (5mm) double-pointed needles
Four stitch markers
Tapestry needle

DIFFICULTY LEVEL:
Medium

SIZES: Small/Medium
(Large/Extra Large)

TO FIT: 22½" (25½)
head circumference

GAUGE

15 sts and 34 rnds = 4" (10cm) in garter st

HAT

Cast on 84 (96) sts using circular needle. Pm and join, being careful not to twist the sts.

Round 1: Knit.

Round 2: Purl.

Repeat rounds 1 and 2 until piece measures 4" (4½).

Shape Crown

Note: Change to dpns when needed.

Next Round: *K21 (24), pm; repeat from * around.

Next Round: Purl.

Decrease round: K2tog, *knit to 3 sts before marker, ssk, k1, sm, k2tog; repeat from * to last 3 sts, ssk, k1—76 (88) sts.

Next Round: Purl.

Next Round: Knit.

Next Round: Purl.

Next Round: Repeat decrease round—68 (80) sts.

Next Round: Purl.

Next Round: Knit.

Repeat last 2 rounds once more.

Next Round: Purl.

Next Round: Repeat decrease round—60 (72) sts.

Next Round: Purl.

Next Round: Knit.

Repeat last 2 rounds once more.

Next Round: Purl.

Next Round: Repeat decrease round—52 (64) sts.

Next Round: Purl.

Next Round: Repeat decrease round—44 (56) sts.

Repeat last 2 rounds 4 times—12 (24) sts.

Next Round: Purl.

Next Round: [K2tog] around—6 (12) sts.

Cut yarn, draw through remaining sts, pull tight, and secure.

Front Brim

Starting at cast-on edge, count 10 sts to one side of first cast-on st. With right side of hat facing you, pick up and knit these 10 sts, then another 10 sts on other side of cast-on st.

Row 1: Knit across, picking up and knitting 1 st at edge of row—21 sts.

Row 2: Knit across, picking up and knitting 1 st at edge of row—22 sts.

Repeat rows 1 and 2 until there are 26 sts.

Next Row: Knit.

Next Row: K1, ssk, knit to last 3 sts, k2tog, k1—24 sts.

Repeat last 2 rows until 16 sts remain.

Next Row: Knit (fold line).

Next Row: Knit.

Next Row: K1, kf&b, knit to last 2 sts, kf&b, k1—18 sts.

Next Row: Knit.

Repeat last 2 rows until there are 26 sts. Bind off, leaving a 10" tail for seaming the brim.

Back Brim

Fold hat in half with Front Brim facing. Turn piece over to back.
Mark the center of the back half of the hat and count 10 sts over from center. Pick up and knit across those 10 sts, then another 10 sts from other side of center. Work as for Front Brim.

Side Flaps

Starting at left edge of Back Brim (at stitch right next to brim), pick up and knit 16 sts, stopping at stitch next to edge of Front Brim.
Knit across for 26 rows.
Decrease row: K1, ssk, knit to last 3 sts, k2tog, k1—14 sts.
Next Row: Knit.

Next Row: Knit.
Next Row: Knit.
Next Row: Repeat decrease row—12 sts.
Knit 3 rows.
Next Row: Repeat decrease row—10 sts.
Next Row: Knit.
Next Row: Repeat decrease row—8 sts.
Next Row: Knit.
Repeat last 2 rows until 4 sts remain.
Next Row: [K2tog] twice—2 sts.
Work in I-cord for 5¼" or desired length.
Bind off.
Repeat on opposite side of hat.
On remaining 2 sts, work I-cord for 5¼" (or desired length).
Bind off.

Finishing

Fold each brim under along "fold line" and seam to edge of hat. Seam sides of brims. Weave in ends. Block.

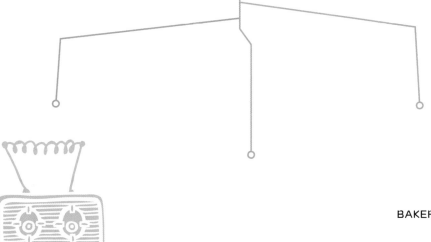

Neil Gaiman

Baker Street scarf

By Joan of Dark

Here's something for a knitter to solve:

What's an easy scarf to knit that looks nice, isn't a basic rib or garter stitch, but can be easily knit while reading a good book or watching a good mystery show? The answer, dear knitter, is the Baker Street Scarf!

Knit in a lovely cashmere yarn that any man (or woman) would want to wear while looking smart around town, the mix of knit and purl on one side and plain knitting on the opposite side give each side of the scarf a cool and unique look. The scarf worn on the BBC version of Sherlock Holmes is in a darker navy or gray color, but since our model is Neil Gaiman, it had to be in black! Make your own version in basic black like Neil's to be mysterious, or in a bright color if standing out in a crowd suits you better!

MATERIALS

Royal Cashmere by Plymouth Yarn Company
    (100% fine cashmere), 1¾ ounce (50g) hanks,
    each approx. 125 yards (114m)
    3 hanks in #8010 Black
Set of size 7 (4.5mm) needles
Size H (5mm) crochet hook

DIFFICULTY LEVEL:
Easy

SIZES: One size

GAUGE

18 stitches and 22 rows = 4" (10cm) in St st

MEASUREMENTS

6" wide and 6' long (after blocking)

SCARF

Cast on 34 sts.

Row 1: K1, p1 across.

Row 2: Knit.

Repeat these two rows until Scarf measures 72".

Bind off.

Finishing

Make fringe: Take a piece of cardboard and cut it down to a 4" square. (You can use an envelope instead of cardboard. Great use for junk mail!)

Wrap the yarn around 20 times and cut on one end.

With crochet hook and starting on corner of one Scarf end, pull 4 pieces of fringe through until both sides are even and tie in a knot.

Do this about every other stitch on Scarf 10 times total. Repeat for other end of Scarf. Block to finish.

TWENTY-SIDED DICE PILLOW

By Joan of Dark

What gamer doesn't want to show off their love of games? Gamers tend to have T-shirts featuring dice, jewelry, clever bags, all sorts of things! So why not pillows to decorate your living room or game room?

This twenty-sided dice pillow is easy to make and easy to roll! Sure, it makes a giant squishy pillow, but it also actually functions the way dice should! Make sure to follow the chart provided when sewing your numbers on and sides together!

MATERIALS

DIFFICULTY LEVEL: Medium

SIZES: One size

128 Superwash by Cascade (100% superwash merino wool), 3½ ounce (100g) hanks, each approx. 128 yards (117m)

    7 skeins in #9486 Shamrock

Set of size 10 (6mm) needles

Polyester fiberfill

Iron-on interfacing

Felt numbers 1–20 (*Note:* If you're crafty, you can make your own!)

Tapestry needle and thread

GAUGE

16 sts and 24 rows = 4" (10cm) in St st

Note: Gauge isn't as critical in this pattern, but consistency is. So take care that your knitting doesn't get looser or tighter with each triangle! Each one needs to be the same size.

John Scalzi and Kristine Scalzi

Twenty-Sided Dice Pillow Chart

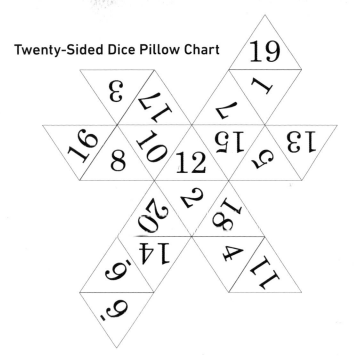

MEASUREMENTS

Each triangle measures 7" on each side.

PILLOW

Triangles

Make twenty.

Cast on 28 sts.

Row 1: Knit.

Row 2: Purl.

Row 3: K2, ssk, k to last 4 sts, k2tog, k2—26 sts.

Row 4: Purl.

Repeat rows 1–4 until 18 sts remain.

Next Row: K2, ssk, k to last 4 sts, k2tog, k2—16 sts.

Next Row: Purl.

Repeat these 2 rows until 8 sts remain.

Next Row: K1, ssk, k2, k2tog, k1.

Next Row: P1, p2tog twice, p1.

Next Row: K2tog twice.

Bind off.

Finishing

Sew numbers onto pieces. Cut and iron interfacing onto the back of each piece. Seam edges together, assembling Triangles using the chart above and stuffing with fiberfill as you work.

John Scalzi and Kristine Scalzi

EIGHT-SIDED DICE PILLOW

By Joan of Dark

Knit in eight pieces then sewn together, you'll need to follow the chart to see how to line the sides up before sewing! Speaking from experience, it's no fun to get your dice sewn together only to realize the 2 is facing the wrong way!

MATERIALS

128 Superwash by Cascade (100% superwash merino wool), 3½ ounce (100g) hanks, each approx. 128 yards (117m)

    4 hanks in #7818 Blue Velvet

Set of size 10 (6mm) needles

Felt numbers 1–8 (*Note:* If you're crafty, you can easily make your own numbers!)

Iron-on interfacing

Tapestry needle

Sewing needle and thread

Polyester fiberfill

DIFFICULTY LEVEL:
Easy

SIZES: One size

GAUGE

16 sts and 24 rows = 4" (10cm) in St st

Note: Gauge isn't as critical in this pattern, but consistency is. So take care that your knitting doesn't get looser or tighter with each side! Each one needs to be the same size.

Eight-Sided Dice Pillow Chart

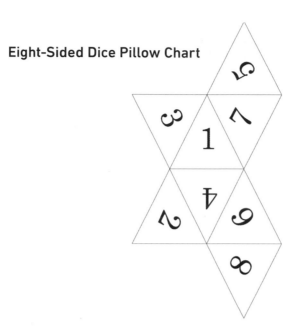

MEASUREMENTS

Each triangle measures 10" on each side.

PILLOW

Triangles

Make eight.

Cast on 40 stitches.

Row 1: Knit.

Row 2: Purl.

Row 3: K2, ssk, knit to last 4 sts, k2tog, k2.
   Row 4: Purl.

Repeat these four rows times—28 sts remain.

Next Row: K2, ssk, knit to last 4 sts, k2tog.

Next Row: Purl.

Repeat these two rows until 8 sts remain.

Next Row: K2, ssk, k2tog, k2—6 sts.

Next Row: P1, p2tog twice p1—4 sts.

Bind off.

Finishing

Sew numbers onto pieces. Cut and iron interfacing onto the back of each piece. Seam edges together, assembling Triangles using the chart above and stuffing with fiberfill as you go.

SIX-SIDED DICE PILLOW

By Joan of Dark

The most easily recognizable shape of dice, this is also the easiest of the dice pillows to make! Knit it in any color to match your room. This pillow goes great in a game room, living room, or bedroom. Like the other dice pillows, it can actually function! Roll it during a real game for fun!

MATERIALS

128 Superwash by Cascade (100% superwash merino wool), 3½ ounce (100g) hanks, each approx. 128 yards (117m)

    7 hanks in #8885 Purple

Set of size 10 (6mm) needles

Felt numbers 1–6 (Note: If you're crafty, you can easily make your own numbers!)

Iron-on interfacing

Tapestry needle

Sewing needle and thread

Polyester fiberfill

DIFFICULTY LEVEL:
Easy

SIZES: One size

GAUGE

14 sts and 22 rows = 4" (10cm) in St st

Note: Like all the other dice pillows, gauge isn't critical. However, make sure to check the width of your square, and knit the height to match! Example: If your square is 12½" across, knit the height to match, instead of the full 13".

Six-Sided Dice Pillow Chart

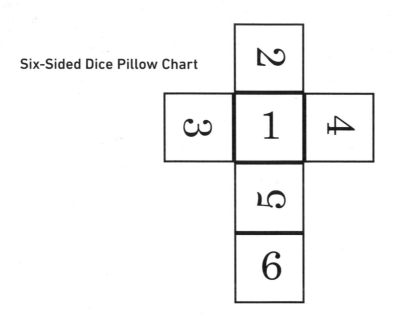

MEASUREMENTS

Each square measures 13" on each side.

PILLOW

Squares

Make six.

Cast on 50 sts.

Row 1: Knit.

Row 2: Purl.

Continue working in St st for 13".

Bind off.

Finishing

Sew numbers to squares of fabric. Cut interfacing to fit square and iron on. Seam edges together following the chart schematic. Before seaming completely, fill with fiberfill, being careful not to overstuff.

John Scalzi and Kristine Scalzi

Kimberlee Moran

DO NOT CROSS   CRIME

keep your pen tie

By Joan of Dark

Sometimes, it can be a real struggle to keep a pen handy. If you're a girl, it's either at the bottom of a giant purse, or you don't carry a purse and have to contend with the fact that, for some inexplicable reason, most girls' clothing comes pocket-free! Since I love wearing ties so much, I decided the best way around this pen/no pocket conundrum would be a tie with a pen holder attached.

Knit in a self-striping retro colors, worked from the bottom up, this tie knits up in a flash. You simply need to know how to increase, decrease, and pick up stitches. It's also a great way to destash some of that extra sock yarn!

MATERIALS

Felici Fingering Self Striping Sock Yarn by Knit Picks
    (75% superwash merino wool, 25% nylon),
    1¾ ounce (50g) balls, each approx. 218 yards (199m)
    1 ball in Building Blocks
Set of size 2 (2.75mm) needles
Tapestry needle

DIFFICULTY LEVEL:
Medium

SIZES: One size

GAUGE

32 sts and 64 rows = 4" (10cm) in garter st

SPECIAL ABBREVIATION

Kf&b: Knit front and back: Knit into the front of the next st as normal but before dropping st off, knit into the back loop of same st, then drop the st from the left needle.

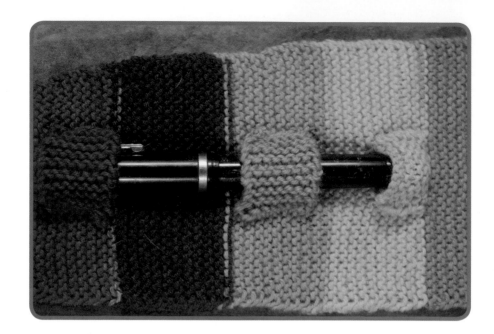

TIE

Cast on 1 st.

Row 1: Kf&b.

Row 2: Kf&b twice—4 sts.

Row 3: K1, kf&b, twice k1—6 sts.

Row 4: Knit.

Row 5: K1, kf&b, knit to last 2 sts, kf&b, k1—8 sts.

Row 6: Knit.

Row 7: K1, kf&b, knit to last 2 sts, kf&b, k1—10 sts.

Repeat rows 6 and 7 until there are 32 sts on the needle.

Knit even until Tie measures 8".

Decrease Row: K1, ssk, knit to last 3 sts, k2tog, k1—30 sts.

Knit even for 3"—total Tie length 11".

Work 1 decrease row—28 sts.

Knit even for 2"—total Tie length 13".

Work 1 decrease row—26 sts.

Knit even for 2"—total Tie length 15".

Work 1 decrease row—24 sts.

Knit even for 2"—total tie length 17".

Work 1 decrease row—22 sts.

Knit even for 1".

Work 1 decrease row—20 sts.

Knit even for 1".

Work 1 decrease row—18 sts.

Knit even for ½".

Work 1 decrease row—16 sts.

Large tie—Knit even for ½".
Work 1 decrease row—14 sts.
Knit even for ½".
Work 1 decrease row—12 sts.
Knit even for ½".
Work 1 decrease row—10 sts.
Knit even across these 10 sts until tie measures 48" long.
Next Row: Work 1 decrease row—8 sts.
Next Row: Knit.
Next Row: Work 1 decrease row—6 sts.
Next Row: Knit.
Next Row: Work 1 decrease row—4 sts.
Next Row: Knit.
Next Row: Work 1 decrease row—2 sts.
Bind off.

PEN HOLDER

Bottom Pocket

On either back or front of Tie, depending on your preference, measure 8" up from bottom of Tie.
Pick up and knit 10 sts centered.
Knit even for ¾".
Bind off.
Seam on two sides, leaving top open.

Center and Top Strap

Measure 1½" from bind off and pick corresponding stripe color (in the case of this tie, blue).
Cast on 8 sts.
Knit 16 rows.
Bind off.
Lay center strap horizontally on stripe, 1½" from bind-off edge of bottom pocket and seam at the cast-on and bind-off edge to Tie.
Measure 1¾" up from top of center strap and pick corresponding stripe color (in the case of this tie, orange). Repeat the process above to make and attach another strap.

Finishing

Weave in ends. Look fashionable and be prepared with a pen ready to go at all times!

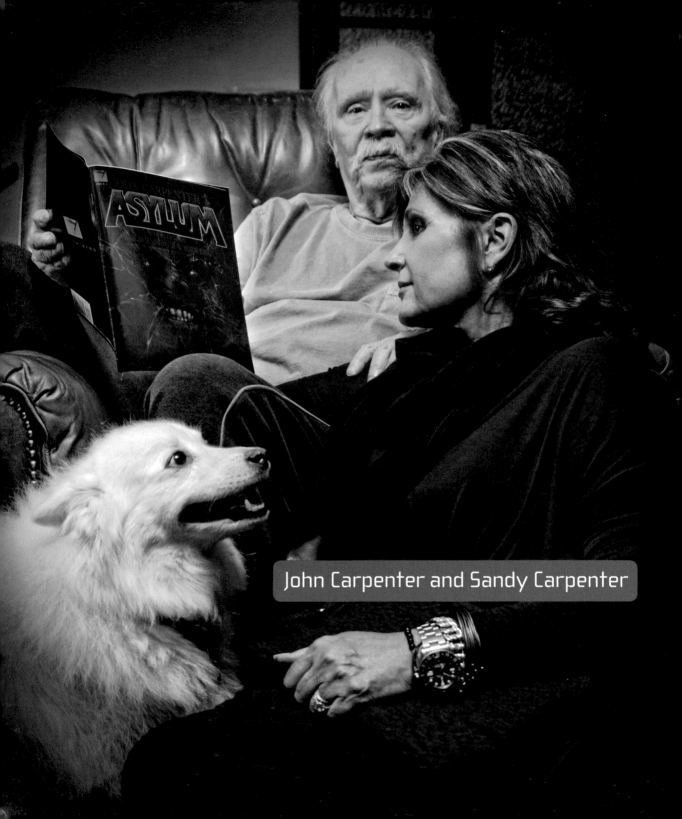

John Carpenter and Sandy Carpenter

COMIC BOOK COVER

By Joan of Dark

This cover is the perfect way to keep your comic safe and sound when carrying it around, either in your hands or in your bag. It's knit with some pretty lacework, then lined with plastic to keep it rigid so your comic won't get bent.

And it's bloodred, since this is being modeled by the master of horror himself, John Carpenter, and his wife, Sandy King Carpenter, who are displaying their comic, *Asylum*!

MATERIALS

Wool of the Andes by Knit Picks (100% Peruvian highland wool), 1¾ ounce (50g) balls, each approx. 110 yards (100m)
    2 balls in Cranberry
Three size 6 (4mm) straight needles (or one pair straight needles and one large stitch holder)
Tapestry needle
Black plastic for insert (plastic canvas used for cross-stitch works very well)
Small button (15mm) or bead

DIFFICULTY LEVEL:
Medium

SIZES: One size

GAUGE

18 sts and 22 rows = 4" (10cm) in St st

COVER

Cast on 80 sts.

Row 1: (RS): K1, ★k1, yo, ssk; repeat from ★ to last st, k1.

Row 2: (WS) K1, purl to last st, k1.

Row 3: K1,★k2, yo, ssk, k2; repeat from ★ to last st, k1.

Row 4: K1, purl to last st, k1.

Row 5: K1, ★k3, yo, ssk, k1; repeat from ★ to last st, k1.

Row 6: K1, purl to last st, k1.

Repeat these 6 rows until piece equals 10¼".

At this point, you will begin working the flap.

Next Row: K2tog, yo, ssk, [k1, yo, ssk] 11 times, ssk, k1. Turn, leaving body on straight needle (or move to st holder), and with new straight needle, begin working on the 38 sts you've just made.

Next row: K1, purl to last st, k1.

Next Row: K2tog, yo, ssk, k2, [k2, yo, ssk, k2] five times, ssk—36 sts.

Next Row: K1, purl to last st, k1.

Next Row: K2tog, k1, yo, ssk, k1, [k3, yo, ssk, k1] four times k2, yo, [ssk] twice—34 sts.

Next Row: K2tog, purl to last 2 sts, k2tog—32 sts.

Next Row: K2tog, [k1, yo, ssk] nine times, k1, ssk—30 sts.

Next Row: K2tog, purl to last 2 sts, k2tog—28 sts.

Next Row: [K2tog] twice, k20, [ssk] twice—24 sts.

Next Row: [K2tog] twice, p16, [k2tog] twice—20 sts.

Next Row: [K2tog] twice, k12, [ssk] twice—16 sts.

Next Row: [K2tog] twice, p8, [k2tog] twice—12 sts.
Next Row: [K2tog] twice, k1, bind off 2, [ssk] twice.
Next Row: K1, p2, cast on 2, p2, k1—8 sts. Bind off.
Join new yarn to live sts and bind off all sts.

Finishing

Cut plastic to fit and with tapestry needle and scrap yarn sew around three edges to create a pocket. Insert into Cover and stitch at bottom two corners to attach.

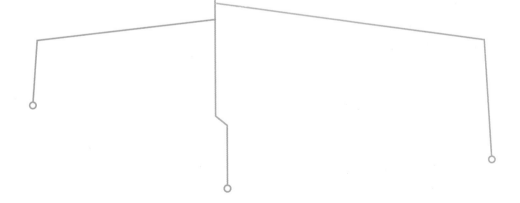

Jennifer Shahade

CHESSBOARD SCARF

By Joan of Dark

Carrying around a chessboard can be a real pain for the chess enthusiast, so why not wear one? This scarf splits a chessboard into two halves. Wrap it around your neck as a warm fashion accessory, then put the two halves together to break into a game!

The pattern is very easy for the beginner knitter, just simple garter stitch with some color changes. As long as your squares are between 2 and 2½", don't stress gauge too much! Twist and tie your color changes on the wrong side of the scarf, then weave in after you're done.

This scarf is done in a classic black-and-white pattern, but you can play around and do light and dark browns as well!

MATERIALS

DIFFICULTY LEVEL: Easy

SIZES: One size

Swish Worsted by Knit Picks (100% superwash
merino wool), 1¾ ounce (50g) balls,
each approx. 110 yards (100m)
11 balls in Black (A)
3 balls in White (B)

Note: If you're careful with the ball, you can get away with just 2 balls of color B. If you leave a longer bit of yarn on your color changes, you will need that third ball. It's about a foot of yarn too short for only using 2 balls.

Set of size 8 (5mm) needles
Tapestry needle or size G (4mm) crochet hook

MEASUREMENTS

10½" in width and 93" in length

GAUGE

22 stitches and 34 rows = 4" (10cm) in
    garter st

SCARF

With A, cast on 48 sts.

Section 1

Row 1 (RS): With B, k12; with A, k12; with
B, k12; with A, k12.

Row 2 (WS): With A, k12; with B, k12; with
A, k12; with B, k12.

Repeat rows 1 and 2 a total of 18 times.

Section 2

Row 3 (RS): With A, k12; with B, k12; with
A, k12; with B, k12.

Row 4 (WS): With B, k12; with A, k12; with
B, k12; with A, k12.

Work rows 3 and 4 a total of 18 times.

Repeat Sections 1 and 2 three more times.

You should have 8 vertical squares.

With A, knit plain for 57" (or longer, if you
desire a longer scarf).

Repeat Sections 1 and 2 as before.

Bind off all sts.

Finishing

Weave in all ends on the wrong side.

acknowledgments

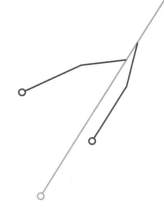

This book has been a very long, very strange journey that would not have been even remotely possible without the help of all my friends and family. First to be thanked must be Lorraine Garland. She introduced me to my agent, Brianne Johnson, who pushed to get this book into the hands of the perfect publisher, St. Martin's Press, where I met BJ and Courtney, who helped me shape the book into the current format. Not only that, Lorraine introduced me to Kyle Cassidy, who agreed to take many red-eye flights and sacrifice lots and lots of sleep to help get the wonderful photos on these pages. (Seriously, a lot of sleep.)

It has to be said that all the models in this book were very gracious and kind to agree to be part of *Geek Knits*. They gave us their time and a teeny bit of their dignity for some of these photos! A special thanks to their wonderful assistants for answering my e-mails, setting up schedules, and making sure we were able to make the photos happen. The crew at Starbase in Indianapolis and the staff at the Marines Memorial Theater in San Francisco were absolutely wonderful about letting us take over spaces and set up for our photo shoots. As was the staff at Starburns, not to mention Rod Hamilton and the amazing Cat Mihos, who went above and beyond to make the Roman Dirge photo shoot happen.

I am grateful to the many talented designers who contributed to this book. You can read all about them in the bios section.

Speaking of designs, a very, very special thank you to James Howe, author of *Bunnicula,* for letting our version of Bunnicula appear in this book. I have now fulfilled my childhood dream of cuddling Bunnicula the Vampire Bunny.

Getting these photos involved a lot of travel, so many thanks to the staff at my coffee shop, Strange Brew, for pitching in and picking up extra shifts. Also pet-sitters extraordinaire, Brandon Lytle, Melissa Kocias, Jeremy Murry, and Russell Sellmeyer.

Cassondra Saxon, aka Deadie Page, for making me look pretty for my author photo. Ditto to Maia Wagle and Chrissy Lynn Kyle for doing Miracle Laurie and Leah Cevoli.

Kerrie Kikendell kept us on point in LA and also drove us around after it was evident that I would have panic attacks if I even attempted to do so. Also my husband, Dan Carr, who makes sure I always get from point A to point B.

And finally, Steve Gosset for being a criminal, Dr. Brad Hafford for grave digging, and Mike Vanhelder for his feet.

Designer Bios

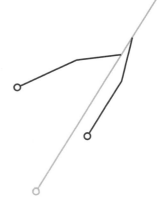

JOAN OF DARK (aka Toni Carr) is an avid lover of all things knit and crocheted. She has been featured on two DIY Network shows, *Uncommon Threads* and *Knitty Gritty*. She's the author of the books *Knockdown Knits* (Wiley) and *Knits for Nerds* (Andrews McMeel), and her patterns have been published on www.KnitPicks.com and in *Vampire Knits* and *Once Upon a Knit* (Potter Craft). When she's not knitting, she's running obstacle races, performing aerial silks, or attending science fiction conventions. You can visit her on the web at www.joanofdark.com.

CLAIRE BOISSEVAIN-CROOKE of Nordic Heart Designs began knitting as a child but didn't become serious about it until moving to a part of the country with real winter, where she discovered stranded color work, graph paper, and steeks.

LAURA HOHMAN is a biologist, Roller Derby girl, and knitter. She lives in the rolling hills of southern Indiana with a husband, one dog, three cats, and some other assorted animals (both wild and semidomesticated). You can find her online at battyknits.blogspot.com. In real life, you can frequently find her at local sci-fantasy conventions, bookstores, microbreweries, or derby bouts.

RILANA RILEY-MUNSON lives, knits, and designs in Portland, Oregon, with an understanding husband, two cats, and an overflowing yarn stash all crammed into a small apartment in the city. When not consuming large quantities of coffee and knitting late into the night, she enjoys reading, loud rock music, and bad-late-night-TV watching.

MARY FITZPATRICK was taught to knit by one of her babysitters when she was in kindergarten, and she's never stopped. She has several day jobs, including naturalist for Great Parks of Hamilton County and exhibit attendant/interpreter for the Insect House at the Cincinnati Zoo. In her spare time, she helps at the Millennicon Science Fiction convention. Making her Alien Pets (see page 31) lets her combine two of her favorite things: knitting and science fiction.

ZABET GROZNAYA (NÉE STEWART) cut her crafting teeth by cofounding TheAntiCraft.com, a punky, geeky, goth-y, pagan-y online craft zine that no longer updates in any regular way. Side effects of said zine have included a sellout (not bestselling!) craft book, *Anticraft: Knitting, Beading, and Stitching for the Slightly Sinister;* new friends all over the Internet; and the opportunity to indulge her massive nerdiness by sitting on geek craft panels at cons. She's currently obsessed with designing stickers and dreams of printing up strange T-shirts for fun and profit.

EMMA BULL came late to knitting, and has been making up for lost time ever since. She writes fantasy and science fiction, including *War for the Oaks, Bone Dance, Territory,* and the free web fiction series Shadow Unit. She knows a thing or two about zombies, having written the mission Living Dead Girl for season two of the popular running app Zombies, Run! And as of print time, Emma is working on a mission for season three! Minneapolis is both her home and her excuse for all this wool.

NOËL MARGARET is a handknit designer and illustrator and is passionate about creating objects and pictures that are interactive and/or tell a story. Noël has exhibited and sold her work in galleries, indie shop, and festivals in New York, Pennsylvania, and Rhode Island. She enjoys sharing her creative-love within her community through teaching, mini-workshops and hosting a knit/crochet group out of her home studio in Upstate New York. You can learn more about Noël by connecting with her on Ravelry at www.ravelry.com/people/NoelMargaret.

CLAIRE REAGAN can't remember a time before knitting. If it weren't for raising two kids, working, and life getting in the way, she would knit 24/7. She loves to transform her ideas into knitting and to spread the knitting fever to others. Find out more about Claire (and her classes and patterns) at claireknits.com.

As a young child, **LINDA J. DUNN** kept getting in the way while her mother knit, so her mother gave her yarn and needles and taught her to cast on, to knit, to bind off, and to stay out of the way while Mother followed a very complicated pattern. During the years since, Linda has been a wife, a seamstress, a clerk-typist, a divorced mom of two, an IU graduate, a published science fiction writer, and a nationally ranked saber fencer. She and her husband live near Indianapolis.

ELIZABETH LOVICK, known as Liz, lives and works on the small Orkney island of Flotta. She has been knitting and designing since she was small and enjoys bringing traditional stitches to modern knitters. Her website is www.northernlace.co.uk, and she sells her patterns on Etsy and Ravelry where she is also northernlace.

GENEVIEVE MILLER is a California girl who's been knitting since she was a child. A teacher on hiatus, she spends her time volunteering at her kids' school, where she helps with all subjects and passes on her love of knitting. Genevieve is the author of *Vampire Knits* and *Once Upon a Knit*. These days, you can find her knitting, geeking out with her husband and three kids, or snapping photos. Follow her at @vampireknits on Twitter and www.genevieveknits@wordpress.com.

MELISSA KOCIAS is an event planner by day, superhero by night, and nerd at all hours. She finds inspiration for her knitting and crochet projects in all sorts of places in time and space.

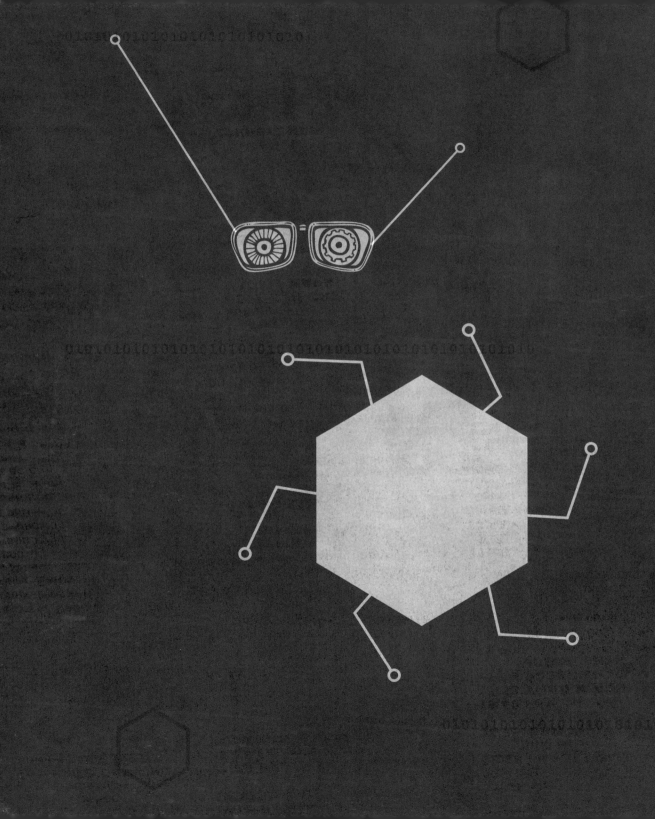

MEET THE AWESOME GEEK KNITS MODELS!

Did you think those models looked familiar? Read below and find out who they are and where you've seen them before!

BONNIE BURTON is the author of the books *The Star Wars Craft Book*, *Draw Star Wars: The Clone Wars*, *Girls Against Girls: Why We Are Mean to Each Other and How We Can Change*, *Star Wars: The Clone Wars: Planets in Peril*, *You Can Draw: Star Wars*, and *Never Threaten to Eat Your Co-Workers: Best of Blogs*, as well as an editor/writer on Womanthology comic from IDW and The Girls' Guide to Guys' Stuff (Friends of Lulu). She currently writes for SFX Magazine and CNET.com. Host of "Ask Bonnie" web series and the *Geek DIY* craft show. She's also the cohost of the Vaginal Fantasy Romance Book Club Show on Geek & Sundry. Learn more on her site Grrl.com.

PAUL AND STORM, otherwise known as Paul Sabourin and Greg "Storm" DiCostanza, are a musical comedy duo. They write songs about geek culture that make people laugh, and because of this, they put together a musical variety show called *W00tstock* with people like Wil Wheaton and Adam Savage. If you want to hear the music of Paul and Storm (highly suggested), check out www.paulandstorm.com.

TRILLIAN STARS (who appears on stage under the name Jennifer Summerfield) is an award-winning actress who has taken on every great role that you might expect, from Olivia in a steampunk version of *Twelfth Night*, to Lady Macbeth, to Josie in *Moon for the Misbegotten*, to Nora in Henrik Ibsen's *A Doll's House*—and when she began running out of the roles you'd expect her to have, she's taken on ones you might not have expected, such as Brutus in *Julius Caesar* and Horatio in *Hamlet*. She also won Best Dressed at the 2009 Hugo Awards.

RENÉ AUBERJONOIS will most likely be recognized by readers of this book for his work on *Star Trek: Deep Space Nine* as Odo. But his résumé is extensive, from the movie version of *M★A★S★H* to Chef Louis in *The Little Mermaid,* and *Warehouse 13,* René doesn't seem to have ever stopped working! Find him at www.renefiles.com.

JOEL HODGSON is well known for his creation of the show *Mystery Science Theater 3000.* Joel played the role of Joel Robinson, who, along with his robot companions, would riff on movies, making some movies unintentionally funny. Joel hasn't stopped riffing on movies. Along with his fellow *MST3K* alums, Joel riffs on movies for live theater and for downloads with *Cinematic Titanic.* Check out Joel on his website, www.joelhodgson.com.

CROW T. ROBOT was built by Joel Robinson and suffers through bad movies alongside Joel and fellow robot Tom Servo. Besides riffing on movies, Crow writes his own screenplays! *Earth vs. Soup, The Spy Who Hugged Me,* and *Chocolate Jones and the Temple of Funk.*

TOM SERVO was also built by Joel Robinson to help Joel and fellow robot Crow battle the madness that can only come from being forced to watch low-quality B movies.

GEORGE R. R. MARTIN is probably best known for *A Game of Thrones* (A Song of Ice and Fire, book 1), the first volume in the cycle of novels that forms the basis for the *Game of Thrones* TV series, but fans were singing his praises long before HBO adapted his books to screen. Go to www.georgerrmartin.com to check out all of his other works!

NEIL GAIMAN is the creator of the popular *Sandman* comics, as well as more books and projects and THINGS than you can shake a stick at. He's also a very nice guy, who has bees and libraries and woods to traipse around in. You can find him at www.neilgaiman.com.

MIRACLE LAURIE is originally from Huntington Beach, California. She's acted in theater since the age of seven and has her BA in drama from the University of California, Irvine. Music, art, and dance have always been a part of her life. Her father is an artist and her mother is a musician/vocalist, as are her two sisters. She has been a part of the Hawaiian community and a Polynesian dancer since she was a child. Miracle modeled for a few years, even appearing on the cover of *Teen Magazine,* and got to work with some great photographers like Bruce Weber. A few years ago, she and her husband fell in love with the ukulele and formed a ukulele duo called Uke Box Heroes (www.ukeboxheroes.com). Miracle feels very blessed to have such a sweet and fun thing in her life and hopes that their fans enjoy it as much as they do.

She was lucky enough to get her big break as "Mellie/November" in Joss Whedon's *Dollhouse* for two seasons. After *Dollhouse* she's been fortunate enough to carve out a small independent film career and has had the pleasure of working right alongside some of the most talented and beloved people in the business, such as Alan Cumming, Garret Dillahunt, Josh Duhamel, Dan Fogler, and Greg Itzen. Miracle also got to reunite with a lot of her *Dollhouse* buddies in the fan-funded film *Lust for Love.*

Miracle enjoys every opportunity she's given in this business and looks forward to the next adventure!

LEAH CEVOLI is not just an actress! Sure, she's been on *Deadwood, My Name Is Earl,* and voiced characters on *Robot Chicken,* but Leah also is a writer, producer, activist, and consultant for those looking to crowdfund projects. In 2012, Leah was voted one of the Most Dangerous Women of Comic-Con, as well as one of the Top Ten Hotties on *Robot Chicken.* When Leah is not acting, hosting, or speaking on panels, she is writing, and is currently a regular staff writer for www.MsInTheBiz.com and www.DailyDead.com.

Currently, she is in preproduction on the feature film *Blood Kiss,* starring Neil Gaiman and Amber Benson, slated to star in J. Lee's fantasy trans-media project *Legendary,* and will be a supporting voice in the new hit cartoon *Bringing Up Tommy,* directed by Fritz Kiersch. Learn more about Leah on her website, www.leahcevoli.com.

JOHN CARPENTER is known as the master of horror for good reason. His movies *Halloween, The Thing,* and *Vampires* hold their own as make-you-hide-under-your-blankets-for-a-week terror flicks! He's also no stranger to the science fiction genre, with flicks like *Starman* and *Escape from New York*. Lately, he's branched into the comic book world with *John Carpenter's Asylum*. You can find him online at www.theofficialjohncarpenter.com.

SANDY KING CARPENTER has worked as a script supervisor, unit manager, and producer. As an artist, she was naturally drawn to the world of comics and helped create *John Carpenter's Asylum*. Besides being ridiculously talented in the world of comics and film, she also makes the best minestrone soup on the planet. You can visit her online at www.stormkingproductions.com.

BOOGIE CARPENTER likes to bark at things and cuddle family and visitors. He's always with his humans, Sandy and John, and helps out during the day working on the *Asylum* comics and making sure the squirrels don't get too close to the avocado tree.

PATRICK ROTHFUSS is a fantasy writer, currently best known for the Kingkiller Chronicles. Patrick writes and blogs on www.patrickrothfuss.com. He founded a really cool charity called Worldbuilders, where geeks come together and help make the world a better place. You can read about it at www.worldbuilders.org.

ADAM SAVAGE is easily recognizable from his show *Mythbusters*. He's also an accomplished costume maker, fabricator, and model maker. As if that weren't enough to keep him busy, Adam is also one of the founders of W00tstock! Check out Adam either on TV or on his website, www.adamsavage.com.

PETER SAGAL is the host of NPR's "Wait, Wait . . . Don't Tell Me!" as well as a writer, a runner, and a screenwriter. He contributes regularly to *Runner's World* magazine, and has a book out called *The Book of Vice: Naughty Things and How to Do Them*. You can check out Peter by being one of the three million listeners who tune into his radio show, or go to his website, www.petersagal.com.

TERYL ROTHERY is recognized by most geeks for her role as Dr. Janet Fraiser on *Stargate SG-1*. She's been in a slew of other roles, lots of them sci-fi, including *Caprica, X-Files,* and *Kyle XY*. Despite an extremely busy acting schedule, Teryl makes time to go to conventions and meet fans! Visit Teryl online at www.terylrothery.com.

WHITNEY AVALON has been a computer geek since the age of four, when her awesome dad (a software engineer) first introduced her to programming languages. She types over 100 WPM and has spent a lot of time down the Internet rabbit hole—so much so that she wrote a song about it. Several puzzles she designed have been published, including in *GAMES Magazine*. In her day job as an actor, she has appeared on *The Big Bang Theory,* sung a trio with Tenacious D, shot a melodrama in an open IKEA store, piloted giant cardboard robots, starred in fifty commercials, and done a lot of other silly things you might have seen. Her original comedy videos (including a series of princess rap battles that includes Leia taking on Galadriel) have been viewed almost 100 million times and cheered by press all over the world. Visit her website, whitneyavalon.com.

JOHN SCALZI and I met at a party at Neil Gaiman's house. He drank Coke Zero like it was going out of style, and a whole bunch of rollergirls covered him in buttercream frosting on the driveway. Just a typical Midwestern party full of writers, really. (Actually, it was for a great charity.) Rollergirls and buttercream frosting isn't his daytime gig, though—he writes awesome books like *Redshirts, The Human Division,* and *Old Man's War*. John is on the web at www.whatever.scalzi.com.

KRISTINE SCALZI is one of the coolest geek girls I know. She can lead you on crazy adventures and has a daughter she is training up for the zombie apocalypse (archery and axe throwing)—and you *really* don't want to use the phrase "fake geek girl" around her. She met John Scalzi when she asked him to dance, and since he is not a stupid man, he said yes.

DAISY SCALZI is a dog. She eats the cat food when John and Kristine aren't looking and hops on the bed even though she isn't supposed to. To make up for it, she gives great cuddles and looks cute on command.

ROMAN DIRGE is best known for his comic series *Lenore*. Roman has also written books like *The Cat with the Really Big Head* and *Something at the Window Is Scratching*. Besides his own projects, he also worked on *Invader Zim* with fellow comic artist Jhonen Vasquez. Roman exists online at www.spookyland.com.

ROSWELL showed up at Kyle Cassidy's back door, six weeks old, feral, and temporarily blind from a bacteria infection, which turned into meningitis. After suffering seizures, she spent a week in kitty ICU, where her vet bills were paid by a concerned crowd of people on the Internet, long before Indiegogo. She recovered splendidly and is now the cat behind morningCATface.com and cookingwithroswell.com. She frequently, and inexplicably, receives gifts of nori, her favorite snack, from strangers on the Internet, for which she is very grateful.

DONNA LYNCH is the cofounder and vocalist of the darkwave band Ego Likeness, and a dark fiction/horror writer and poet. She lives in Maryland with her husband, artist/musician/author Steven Archer (also pictured). She is found on the web at www.egolikeness.com.

Besides being a fan of **RODNEY ANONYMOUS,** also known as Rodney Linderman, as the lead vocalist and keyboard player for the Dead Milkmen, I got to know him as someone oddly fascinated with Jane Austen–themed knitwear. Rodney writes for the *Philadelphia City* paper and on his website, www.rodneyanonymous.com.

DREW CURTIS is the founder/CEO/sole owner of Kentucky-based Fark.com—the Internet's primary source for not-news (and news) that happens to be humorous since

1999. Some highlights from the past fifteen years include *It's Not News, It's Fark: How Mass Media Passes Off Crap as News,* a book even more relevant today than ever; having a Fark category on *Jeopardy!*—twice; being sued by a patent troll and getting a TED talk out of it: *How I Beat a Patent Troll*; and co-creating Stone Farkin Wheaton W00tstout, a Stone Brewing Collaboration ale, with Drew, Greg Koch, and Wil Wheaton.

JENNIFER SHAHADE is a chess champion, author, poker player, and commentator. Besides being a two-time American Women's Chess Champion, she is also the Mind Sports Ambassador at Poker Stars. Go to www.jennifershahade.com to learn all the awesome things about Jennifer!

KIMBERLEE SUE MORAN has been a forensic consultant and educator since 2002, both in the UK and the United States. Kimberlee has worked on a number of cases in a range of capacities; she runs training workshops for local law enforcement that include blowing up transit buses and digging up dead animals. Her doctoral research was in the field of ancient fingerprints and her current research is in taphonomy, the process of decomposition. Kimberlee is passionate about outreach and science education and is a regular participant and speaker for the Philadelphia Science Festival working in collaboration with the Mütter Museum and the Laurel Hill Cemetery. She is an active member of the Society for American Archaeology, the UK Fingerprint Society, the Association for Women in Forensic Science, and Forensic Archaeology Recovery. Kimberlee holds an undergraduate degree in archaeology from Bryn Mawr College and a Masters of Science in forensic archaeological science from the Institute of Archaeology at University College London. She was also the "Geekadelphia" Scientist of the year.

INDEX

Alien Pet, *30,* 31–32, *33,* 34–35
Alien Snow Beast Balaclava, *42,* 43–46, *47*
America! Sweater Dress, *98,* 99–103, *101–3*
Anderson-Corwin, Noel
    Dire Wolf, *104,* 105–6, *107,* 108–13
    Dragon, *72,* 73–84, *75, 80–81*
animals
    Alien Snow Beast Balaclava, *42,* 43–46, *47*
    Bunnicula, *122,* 123–28, *125–26, 129–31,* 165
    Carpenter, B., 174
    Dire Wolf, *104,* 105–6, *107,* 108–13
    Dragon, *72,* 73–84, *75, 80–81*
    Helpful Worm, *56,* 57–62, *63*
    Roswell, *16,* 176
    Scalzi, D., *148,* 176
    Where No Dog (or Cat) has Gone Before, *16,*
        17–18, *19,* 20–21
Anonymous, Rodney (Rodney Linderman), *36,* 176
Asylum!, 158, 159
Auberjonois, René, *26,* 172
Avalon, Whitney, *98,* 99, *102,* 175

Bad Robot Fingerless Gloves, *12,* 13–15, *15*
Baker Street Hat, *138,* 139–41
Baker Street Scarf, *142,* 143–44, *144*
Batman comics, 95
Blue Box Scarf, *26,* 27–28, *29*
Boissevain-Crooke, Claire, 167
    Muggle Artifact Sweater, *64,* 65–67, *67–71, 70–71*
Bow Ties are Cool, *52,* 53–54, *54*
Broken Blade Hooded Sweater, *118,* 119–21, *120–21*
Bull, Emma, 168

Running Dead Headband and Hat, The, *132,*
    133–36, *134–35*
Bunnicula, *122,* 123–28, *125–26, 129–31,* 165
Burton, Bonnie, *2, 5, 86,* 171

Carpenter, Boogie, 174
Carpenter, John, *158,* 159, 173–74
Carpenter, Sandy King, *158,* 159, 174
Carr, Dan, 166
Carr, Toni. *See* Joan of Dark
Cassidy, Kyle, x, 165
Cevoli, Leah, *94,* 173
Chessboard Scarf, *162,* 163–64, *164*
clothes
    Alien Snow Beast Balaclava, *42,* 43–46, *47*
    Bad Robot Fingerless Gloves, *12,* 13–15, *15*
    Baker Street Hat, *138,* 139–41
    Baker Street Scarf, *142,* 143–44, *144*
    Blue Box Scarf, *26,* 27–28, *29*
    Broken Blade Hooded Sweater, *118,* 119–21,
        120–21
    Chessboard Scarf, *162,* 163–64, *164*
    Companion Scarf, *2,* 2–4, *5*
    Cthulhu Fingerless Gloves, 89, *90,* 91–92, *92–93*
    Fezzes are Cool, *48,* 49–59
    Muggle Artifact Sweater, *64,* 65–67, *67–71, 70–71*
    Running Dead Headband and Hat, The, *132,*
        133–36, *134–35*
    Time Traveler Socks, *36,* 37–40, *41*
    Verse Sweater, *6,* 7–8, *9,* 10–11, *11*
    Where No Dog (or Cat) has Gone Before, *16,*
        17–18, *19,* 20–21

Comic Book Cover, *158,* 159–61, *160–61*
comic conventions, ix–x
Communicator Purse, *22,* 23–25, *24–25*
Companion Scarf, *2,* 2–4, *5*
Crow T. Robot, *30,* 172
Cthulhu Fingerless Gloves, 89, *90,* 91–92, *92–93*
Curtis, Drew, 176–77

DiCostanza, Greg "Storm." *See* Storm
difficulty. *See* easy level; hard level; medium level
Dire Wolf, *104,* 105–6, *107,* 108–13
Dirge, Roman, *118, 120,* 165, 176
Dragon, *72,* 73–84, *75, 80–81*
Dragon Rider Shrug, *114,* 115–17, *117*
Dunn, Linda J., 169
　　Alien Snow Beast Balaclava, *42,* 43–46, *47*
　　America! Sweater Dress, *98,* 99–103, *101–3*

easy level, x
　　Baker Street Scarf, *142, 143–44, 144*
　　Blue Box Scarf, *26,* 27–28, *29*
　　Chessboard Scarf, *162,* 163–64, *164*
　　Eight-Sided Dice Pillow, *146, 148,* 149–50, *150, 153*
　　Six-Sided Dice Pillow, *146,* 151–52, *152–53*
Eight-Sided Dice Pillow, *146, 148,* 149–50, *150, 153*
everyday geeks, 137
　　Baker Street Hat, *138,* 139–41
　　Baker Street Scarf, *142,* 143–44, *144*
　　Chessboard Scarf, *162,* 163–64, *164*
　　Comic Book Cover, *158,* 159–61, *160–61*
　　Eight-Sided Dice Pillow, *146, 148,* 149–50, *150, 153*
　　Keep Your Pen Tie, *154,* 155–57, *156*
　　Six-Sided Dice Pillow, *146,* 151–52, *152–53*
　　Twenty-Sided Dice Pillow, 145, *146–47,* 147, *153*

Fair Isle tips, 134–35
Fallen Blade series (McCullough), 119
fantasy geeks, 55
　　America! Sweater Dress, *98,* 99–103, *101–3*
　　Broken Blade Hooded Sweater, *118,* 119–21, *120–21*
　　Bunnicula, *122,* 123–28, *125–26, 129–31,* 165

Cthulhu Fingerless Gloves, 89, *90,* 91–92, *92–93*
Dire Wolf, *104,* 105–6, *107,* 108–13
Dragon, *72,* 73–84, *75, 80–81*
Dragon Rider Shrug, *114,* 115–17, *117*
Helpful Worm, *56,* 57–62, *63*
Intern Cowl, *86,* 87–88
Muggle Artifact Sweater, *64,* 65–67, *67–71,* 70–71
Poison Ivy Wrap, *94,* 95–97
Running Dead Headband and Hat, The, *132,* 133–36, *134–35*
Fezzes are Cool, *48,* 49–59
Firefly, 7
Fitzpatrick, Mary, 168
　　Alien Pet, *30,* 31–32, *33,* 34–35

Gaiman, Neil, *138, 142,* 143, 172
Garland, Lorraine, 165
geeks, ix–x. *See also* everyday geeks; fantasy geeks; science fiction geeks
gloves, 4, *4*
　　Bad Robot Fingerless Gloves, *12,* 13–15, *15*
　　Cthulhu Fingerless Gloves, 89, *90,* 91–92, *92–93*
Groznaya, Zabet, 168
　　Helpful Worm, *56,* 57–62, *63*

Hamilton, Rod, 165
hard level, x
　　Cthulhu Fingerless Gloves, 89, *90,* 91–92, *92–93*
　　Muggle Artifact Sweater, *64,* 65–67, *67–71,* 70–71
　　Running Dead Headband and Hat, The, *132,* 133–36, *134–35*
Harry Potter and the Goblet of Fire (Rowling), 65
hats
　　Alien Snow Beast Balaclava, *42,* 43–46, *47*
　　Baker Street Hat, *138,* 139–41
　　Fezzes are Cool, *48,* 49–59
　　Running Dead Headband and Hat, The, *132,* 133–36, *134–35*
Helpful Worm, *56,* 57–62, *63*
Hodgson, Joel, 172
Hohman, Laura, 167
　　Bad Robot Fingerless Gloves, *12,* 13–15, *15*
　　Time Traveler Socks, *36,* 37–40, *41*
Holmes, Sherlock, 139

Howe, James, 123, 165

Intern Cowl, *86*, 87–88
Isley, Pamela (Poison Ivy), 95

Joan of Dark (Carr, Toni), ix–x, 167
    Baker Street Hat, *138*, 139–41
    Baker Street Scarf, *142*, 143–44, *144*
    Bow Ties are Cool, *52*, 53–54, *54*
    Broken Blade Hooded Sweater, *118*, 119–21,
        120–21
    Chessboard Scarf, *162*, 163–64, *164*
    Comic Book Cover, *158*, 159–61, *160–61*
    Companion Scarf, *2*, 2–4, *5*
    Dragon Rider Shrug, *114*, 115–17, *117*
    Eight-Sided Dice Pillow, *146*, *148*, 149–50, *150*,
        153
    Fezzes are Cool, *48*, 49–59, *51*
    Intern Cowl, *86*, 87–88
    Keep Your Pen Tie, *154*, 155–57, *156*
    Six-Sided Dice Pillow, *146*, 151–52, *152–53*
    Twenty-Sided Dice Pillow, 145, *146–47*, 147, *153*
    Verse Sweater, *6*, 7–8, *9*, 10–11, *11*
Johnson, Brianne, 165

Keep Your Pen Tie, *154*, 155–57, *156*
Kikendell, Kerrie, 166
Knits for Nerds (Carr), 167
Knockdown Knits (Carr), 167
Kocias, Melissa, 169
    Blue Box Scarf, *26*, 27–28, *29*

Labyrinth, 57
Laurie, Miracle, *9*, 172–73
    Dragon Rider Shrug, *114*, *117*
Linderman, Rodney. *See* Anonymous, Rodney
Lovick, Elizabeth, 169
    Where No Dog (or Cat) has Gone Before, *16*,
        17–18, *19*, 20–21
Lynch, Donna, *12*, 176

Marines Memorial Theater (San Francisco), 165
Martin, George R. R., *104*, 105, 172
McCullough, Kelly, 119

medium level, x
    Alien Pet, *30*, 31–32, *33*, 34–35
    Alien Snow Beast Balaclava, *42*, 43–46, *47*
    America! Sweater Dress, *98*, 99–103, *101–3*
    Bad Robot Fingerless Gloves, *12*, 13–15
    Baker Street Hat, *138*, 139–41
    Bow Ties are Cool, *52*, 53–54, *54*
    Broken Blade Hooded Sweater, *118*, 119–21,
        120–21
    Bunnicula, *122*, 123–28, *125–26*, *129–31*, 165
    Comic Book Cover, *158*, 159–61, *160–61*
    Communicator Purse, *22*, 23–25, *24–25*
    Companion Scarf, *2*, 2–4, *5*
    Dire Wolf, *104*, 105–6, *107*, 108–13
    Dragon, *72*, 73–84, *75*, *80–81*
    Dragon Rider Shrug, *114*, 115–17, *117*
    Fezzes are Cool, *48*, 49–59
    Helpful Worm, *56*, 57–62, *63*
    Intern Cowl, *86*, 87–88
    Keep Your Pen Tie, *154*, 155–57, *156*
    Poison Ivy Wrap, *94*, 95–97
    Time Traveler Socks, *36*, 37–40, *41*
    Twenty-Sided Dice Pillow, 145, *146–47*, 147, *153*
    Verse Sweater, *6*, 7–8, *9*, 10–11, *11*
    Where No Dog (or Cat) has Gone Before, *16*,
        17–18, *19*, 20–21
Mihos, Cat, 165
Miller, Genevieve, 169
    Communicator Purse, *22*, 23–25, *24–25*
Moran, Kimberlee, *154*, 177
Muggle Artifact Sweater, *64*, 65–67, *67–71*, *70–71*

Noël, Margaret, 168

Paul and Storm, *56*, 171. *See also* Storm
Poison Ivy. *See* Isley, Pamela
Poison Ivy Wrap, *94*, 95–97
purse, *22*, 23–25, *24–25*

Reagan, Claire, 169
    Bunnicula, *122*, 123–28, *125–26*, *129–31*, 165
Riley-Munson, Rilana, *94*, 95–97, 167
robots
    Bad Robot Fingerless Gloves, *12*, 13–15

Crow T. Robot, *30, 172*
Tom Servo, *25, 172*
Roswell, *16, 176*
Rothery, Teryl, *90, 175*
Rothfuss, Patrick, *174*
Rowling, J. K., 65
Running Dead Headband and Hat, The, *132,* 133–36, *134–35*

Sabourin, Paul. *See* Paul and Storm
Savage, Adam, *64, 72, 174*
Saxon, Cassondra, 166
Scalzi, Daisy, *148, 176*
Scalzi, John, *146, 148, 153,* 175
Scalzi, Kristine, *146, 148, 153,* 175
scarves
    Baker Street Scarf, *142,* 143–44, *144*
    Blue Box Scarf, *26,* 27–28, *29*
    Chessboard Scarf, *162,* 163–64, *164*
    Companion Scarf, *2,* 2–4, *5*
science fiction conventions, ix–x
science fiction geeks, 1
    Alien Pet, *30,* 31–32, *33,* 34–35
    Alien Snow Beast Balaclava, *42,* 43–46, *47*
    Bad Robot Fingerless Gloves, *12,* 13–15
    Blue Box Scarf, *26,* 27–28, *29*
    Bow Ties are Cool, *52,* 53–54, *54*
    Communicator Purse, *22,* 23–25, *24–25*
    Companion Scarf, *2,* 2–4, *5*
    Fezzes are Cool, *48,* 49–59
    Time Traveler Socks, *36,* 37–40, *41*
    Verse Sweater, *6,* 7–8, *9,* 10–11, *11*
    Where No Dog (or Cat) has Gone Before, *16,* 17–18, *19,* 20–21
Sagal, Peter, *132*
Shahade, Jennifer, *162, 164,* 177
Six-Sided Dice Pillow, *146,* 151–52, *152–53*
socks, *36,* 37–40, *41*
Star Trek: The Next Generation, ix
Starbase (Indianapolis), 165
Stars, Trillian, *6,* 171
Storm (DiCostanza, Greg "Storm"), *56, 63,* 171
Strange Brew, 165–66
Summerfield, Jennifer. *See* Stars, Trillian

sweaters
    Broken Blade Hooded Sweater, *118,* 119–21, *120–21*
    Muggle Artifact Sweater, *64,* 65–67, *67–71,* 70–71
    Verse Sweater, *6,* 7–8, *9,* 10–11, *11*
    Where No Dog (or Cat) has Gone Before, *16,* 17–18, *19,* 20–21

Thor movies, 87
Time Traveler Socks, *36,* 37–40, *41*
Tom Servo, *25, 172*
toys
    Alien Pet, *30,* 31–32, *33,* 34–35
    Bunnicula, *122,* 123–28, *125–26, 129–31,* 165
    Dire Wolf, *104,* 105–6, *107,* 108–13
    Dragon, *72,* 73–84, *75, 80–81*
    Eight-Sided Dice Pillow, *146, 148,* 149–50, *150, 153*
    Helpful Worm, *56,* 57–62, *63*
    Six-Sided Dice Pillow, *146,* 151–52, *152–53*
    Twenty-Sided Dice Pillow, 145, *146–47, 147, 153*
Twenty-Sided Dice Pillow, 145, *146–47, 147, 153*

Vanhelder, Mike, 166
Verse Sweater, *6,* 7–8, *9,* 10–11, *11*

Weasleys, 65
Where No Dog (or Cat) has Gone Before, *16,* 17–18, *19,* 20–21